Cultural Survival Report 27

INDIGENOUS PEOPLES AND TROPICAL FORESTS

Models of Land Use and Management from Latin America

Jason W. Clay

Cultural Survival, Inc.
Cambridge, Massachusetts

With assistance from the Public Welfare Foundation,
the Ford Foundation and the US Man and Biosphere Program

Cultural Survival, Inc.
53-A Church Street
Cambridge, MA 02138
(617) 495-2562

1st Reprinting December 1990

Printed in the United States of America
by Transcript Printing Company,
Peterborough, NH

Cultural Survival Report 27
The Cultural Survival Report is a continuation of
the Occasional Paper series.

Cover: Photo of Yanomamo Indian, Venezuela, by Napoleon A. Chagnon.

Library of Congress Cataloging-in-Publication Data
Clay, Jason W.
    Indigenous peoples and tropical forests : models of land use and management from
    Latin America / Jason W. Clay   p.   cm. — (Cultural survival report : 27)
    Bibliography: p.   ISBN 0-939521-38-5 : $19.95.   ISBN 0-939521-32-6 (pbk.) : $8.00
    1. Rain forest ecology—Latin America.   2. Land use—Latin America.   3. Indians of
    Central America—Land tenure.   4. Indians of South America—Land tenure.   I.
    Title   II. Series.
    GF514.C56 1988
    304.2 '5 '098--dc19   88-28518
                                                                                      CIP

Printed on recycled paper

Preface

This report is divided into categories traditionally used to describe the types of research undertaken on resource management activities of indigenous peoples — fishing, hunting, gathering, shifting cultivation and so on. These categories rarely represent distinct activities in real life, let alone theoretical categories for those pursuing them. A more holistic approach, emphasizing a specific group's economic activities, would have avoided the compartmentalization of activities but would have narrowed the report's scope over comparative material. It is also my contention that, at best, specific activities or general principles can be transferred from one indigenous group to another or to colonists. An in-depth focus on a few specific groups would have offered fewer insights into the problems these groups face or some of the solutions they are attempting to uncover.

Throughout the report, I have attempted to show how the specific economic activities singled out for scrutiny by researchers are being modified in response to economic, social, population and political pressures. This is not to imply that traditional resource management strategies have been abandoned, just that they now exist side by side with modified traditional systems. When indigenous peoples modify traditional resource management/use practices, they produce some of the most interesting economic and environmental experiments being undertaken in rain forests.

This unending and extraordinarily original experimentation, occurring as it does with each individual of each group, offers the most hope not only for the groups' continued survival but that of the forests and perhaps other groups as well.

The term *rain forests* appears throughout the text, despite the fact that some of the examples are from dry rather than humid tropical areas; to be more specific in these descriptions would confuse a general audience. Readers should keep in mind, however, that tropical forest environments, even rain forests, vary tremendously. These variations are extremely important not only for their fragility in the face of human occupation and present management strategies, but also future modification of such systems.

The research for this book began in 1984 and was completed, for the most part, the following year. Since that time, additions have been made both to the text and to the references section, but no thorough effort has been made to keep abreast of the increasing amounts of literature being published on the topics covered in the report. The report includes enough of the people doing the research on the forefront of these issues, as well as the titles of journals that regularly publish current research on these topics, that it will be easy enough for researchers to pursue further any of the topics.

The references section was originally divided into a number of subsections which reflected the various parts of this book as well as works on such general topics as tropical ecology; development, tropical agriculture and ecology; shifting cultivation; agroforestry; and research on indigenous/traditional agroforestry systems. As I was attempting to show what was known about similar practices in other parts of the world, each of these sections was further divided in geographical areas. The first people to review the manuscript objected to the compartmentalization of the bibliography, saying that readers would have difficulty finding the references that were cited in the text. For that reason, I have alphabetized all references by author. Readers must now read the references section line by line for those more general works or geographically specialized works that are not cited in the text.

One of the primary difficulties in preparing this report was in assessing the role of indigenous peoples as conservationists; or, put another way, in attempting to distinguish between those people who *use* resources and those who *manage* them. Anthropologists, who have done most research on the economic activities of indigenous peoples in Latin America, frequently err on the side of romanticism in their views of Indians as "the once and future resource managers." Biologists and conservationists, by contrast, are often adamant that unless the peoples articulate a conscious intent regarding specific resource utilization practices, these practices should fall under "sustainable resource use," not "sustainable resource management."

This basic distinction can be — and is — debated for hours. However, the polarization, not to mention the endless debate, is not terribly useful. The ways in which resources are utilized on all but a tiny fraction of European and North American farms is not sustainable, but yet they are highly managed. Some practices are accepted as conservationist without an understanding of their "scientific" basis. Indigenous people, because of the romanticism that surrounds what is often assumed to be their pristine lifestyles, appear to be being forced to adhere to a different standard than everyone else. What we are talking about are resource utilization systems that are in relatively sustainable stasis with the environment. It is safe to say that the lifestyle of any conservationist, at least one that lives in the industrialized parts of the world, is less sustainable from an environmental point of view than that of an indigenous person who happens to live in the "front line" of environmental destruction in the tropics.

Indigenous peoples are not conservationists in the same way as we all too infrequently try to be; for example, they rarely attempt to get other peoples' houses in order. The various world views and beliefs about the environment that distinguish indigenous peoples from us as well as from each other lead to specific systems of resource management. These systems are rarely random or even mostly opportunistic. The belief systems and the actions that are central to these systems represent attempts to maintain order in the world. Some of them are sustainable; some are not. Some are sustainable under certain conditions, but become destructive under others. Some individuals are more conserving than others in the same group. This is not terribly different than in our own societies.

The question that comes to mind, then, is: which conditions will encourage more indigenous people living in fragile environments to conserve resources? One of the most important issues underscored in this report is the ability of indigenous peoples to organize themselves both to work with those who would support them and against those who would eliminate them. Strong organizations allow indigenous peoples to focus on other issues that are also key to their survival — the local autonomy and the information necessary to make decisions that affect the future: secure land rights and sources of income which complement the environment and lifestyles of the local inhabitants.

One major issue which is discussed only in passing in this review is the relationship of insatiable consumption patterns and non-suitable resource utilization practices in industrialized countries to the world's fragile rainforest systems. As we work to understand how indigenous peoples survive in fragile habitats, we must renew our efforts to halt or reduce those practices closer to home that threaten the world's rain forests and their inhabitants.

Acknowledgments

This review was funded by the US Man and Biosphere Program, Directorate on Tropical and Sub-Tropical Forests, to help focus attention on critical issues affecting humans living in the tropics. Publication of the review was made possible, in part, by a grant from the Public Welfare Foundation.

I would like to thank Marianne Schmink and Ariel Lugo for their support in getting this project off the ground and their patience while waiting for the final product. I would also like to thank the hundreds of researchers who offered advice during the research. In particular, I would like to thank those who offered substantial comments on the scope of the project or earlier drafts: Sondra Wentzel, Mac Chapin, Jean-Claude Faby, W. Finlayson, Terese Butler Hart, John Hart, Dominique Irvine, Carl Jordan, Mark Leighton, Peter Murphy, P. K. R. Nair, James Nations, Christine Padoch, Darrell Posey, Antonio Viera and Christopher Uhl. Their comments and suggestions were invaluable; I alone am responsible for any shortcomings in the final product.

I would like to thank, too, Gwyn Gallagher for typing and making changes on the manuscript, Ruth Taswell and Leslie Baker for their careful and constructive editing and Alexa Schulz for drawing all figures.

This book is dedicated to those indigenous peoples who are presently attempting to keep body and soul together in a rapidly changing world through their innovative resource management efforts. This book, in its own small way, tries to show where we might draw insight as well as inspiration from their efforts.

Contents

List of Figures

Introduction

The exploitation of tropical rain forests in Latin America varies over time and from one region to another. In Central America, for example, it appears to have eased in the last decade as a result of the number and duration of military conflicts. In the Amazon basin, however, rainforest exploitation has continued at the same level or has even intensified. Rising international debts and poor investment returns in the late 1960s and early 1970s caused a decline in domestic and private funding of massive road-building and colonization projects. Multilateral and bilateral international funding for such projects has continued well into the 1980s, however, often picking up where local governments had abandoned their efforts.

In Latin America, unlike other parts of the world, the main damage done to rainforest areas does not result from logging or cutting fuelwood although these are increasingly problems in some areas. Rather, it results from agricultural activities. In some areas of Latin America, such as parts of Central America and Brazil, the most accessible tropical rain forests had already been converted to cropland or pasture by the 1980s; the remaining land was relatively remote or of extremely poor quality. By the late 1970s, scientists, agriculturalists and planners had begun to document systematically the consequences of development efforts in tropical rain forests. Their research called into question the assumptions and hopes of many government officials: that these remote and seemingly unused areas would alleviate resource shortages.

By the mid-1980s, many governments became convinced that certain areas of tropical rain forests are unsuitable for even limited use. Only a small area within tropical rain forests can be safely exploited through intensive agriculture. A larger area can only be exploited in a limited fashion. Few, if any, areas of tropical rain forests can be converted to agricultural production following the strategies imported from mid-latitude regions for annual, cereal crops. Unfortunately, the international debts that have slowed the organized expansion of agricultural production systems into many regions of tropical rain forests are now fueling a desperate search for riches in these same areas — governments, and their international backers, are looking for a "quick fix" to their financial hardships.

In addition to spawning "get rich quick" efforts in tropical rain forests, international debts also are responsible for creating government programs and incentives for massive mining and hydroelectric complexes and large-scale, high-input farming. Some of these programs — for example, mechanized soybean production in southern Brazil — have led to agricultural production shifts that displace large numbers of former tenants or sharecroppers in non-rainforest regions; these displaced people, in turn, look to so-called uninhabited rain forests not so much for their future but as their last hope. In Central America, the conversion of former food-producing, labor-intensive production systems to livestock or cash crop production systems has displaced a number of landless people into fragile rainforest areas.

In the past 25 years, various Latin American governments financed colonization projects in rainforest areas. These projects were inevitably funded by other countries, in particular the United States, or multilateral banks such as the World Bank or the Inter-American Development Bank. In spite of these massive colonization projects, most colonists in Latin America migrated without government assistance, although they continue to pressure their respective governments to provide basic goods and services in their new habitats and, more importantly, land titles and security.

Agricultural production and land tenure systems, which have evolved since Western colonization of rainforest areas, cannot accommodate, without modification, expanding populations. Tropical rain forests, often referred to simply as the "frontier," have long been used as a safety valve for expanding populations. Recently, rain forests became the focus of nationally and internationally funded research with multiple goals: increase the foreign exchange earnings of many Latin American countries, absorb populations (thereby reducing political unrest) and generate food supplies for urban areas. Much of the research has focused on how to sponsor development in tropical rain forests without destroying their potential as a resource base for future generations. Millions of dollars have been spent on identifying areas of tropical rain forests that can best accommodate the expansion of existing systems of agricultural production or that are most suitable for the extraction of minerals, hydroelectric power or timber. Research efforts have stressed the potential of specific crops — both local and imported — that might alone or in combination with other known species generate income in tropical rainforest areas.

To date, those development projects based on forest clearing and the subsequent establishment of large-scale cattle ranches or vast farms devoted to the cultivation of monocultures or a limited number of cash crops have been ecological failures and, in most cases, economic failures as well. (They are economic failures *in most cases* because some of the large-scale banana, cacao, coffee, rubber or cotton plantations *may* be economically viable; however, little research exists on the economic viability or social costs of such ventures.) Most observers acknowledge the need to minimize the negative, long-term or permanent impact of development efforts on tropical rain forests, yet they also recognize the urgency of developing sensible uses for tropical rain forests. These regions face the danger of being destroyed through uncontrolled development efforts — a possibility that grows increasingly immi-

Thin cattle replace dense rain forests in eastern Chiapas, Mexico.   ©J. Nations

nent as Latin American governments face serious economic, and possibly political, crises.

Until now, few researchers have examined the ways indigenous inhabitants of tropical rain forests use and sustain their region's resources (for notable exceptions, see Conklin 1957 and Harris 1971 on shifting cultivation; Covich and Nickerson 1966 on house gardens; Posey 1982a, 1983a on forest and trail side fields). Nations and Komer (1983) suggest that such research could provide guidelines for development in Latin America's tropical rain forests that would benefit colonists and government alike.

> By combining the ecologically sound, sustainable yield principles of Indian agriculture with specific techniques of commercial agriculture, researchers are creating new production systems that can improve the lives of rainforest colonists and conserve forest resources at the same time.

Posey et al. (1984:104) echo these views, suggesting

> the need for systematic study of indigenous systems of knowledge and utilization of the Amazonian ecosystems. It appears that such study can contribute to the formulation of ecologically sound, efficiently productive, profitable, labor-intensive and integrated management systems of agriculture, aquaculture, and the cropping of wild and semidomesticated plants, mammals, fish, reptiles, birds and insects. Besides being commercially productive, such systems would blend with the natural Amazonian ecosystems, thereby preserving the

diverse natural genetic stock with its own unknown potential for commodities with nutritional, medicinal, and industrial use.

Through the centuries, indigenous peoples living in the tropical rain forests of the Western Hemisphere have developed sustained-yield subsistence systems which often combine root crops, vegetable crops and select tree crops and, in turn, improve hunting, fishing and gathering. More recently, cash or marketable crops and pastures have been added to the mix. While adoption of these systems utilized by indigenous peoples, in toto, is not always socially or economically acceptable for immigrant populations in these areas, the study of the existing indigenous agro-ecosystems nevertheless provides a better understanding of the internal dynamics, and perhaps limits, of complex ecosystems.

Not surprisingly, the indigenous societies in these tropical regions are becoming extinct at an even faster rate than the regions they have traditionally inhabited. In many indigenous societies undergoing rapid change, young people no longer learn the methods by which their ancestors maintained fragile regions. Little time remains to salvage this knowledge upon which "new strategies for ecologically and socially sound sustained yield development" (Posey et al. 1984:104) might be based.

This report summarizes the research on six activities pursued by indigenous peoples in rainforest areas of Central and South America that sustain both their own populations and the environment: gathering, hunting, fishing, shifting agriculture, permanent agriculture and "upgrading" of natural resource/forest bases. Each of these sections includes one or more cases describing how indigenous peoples are attempting to modify their activities to increase their cash income while ensuring that the resource management activities are sustainable over the long term. A list of research priorities appears at the end of each section. The report then discusses three cases of large-scale land use management that involve indigenous peoples and fragile ecosystems. Finally, the report discusses the overall implications and the limitations of this research for developing models of sustained economic use of tropical rain forests in Latin America.

Three main questions arise when attempting to determine if indigenous management practices in tropical rain forests are appropriate management models for indigenous or colonist populations. First, can indigenous management practices related to specific belief systems be converted to acceptable conservation axioms that will also be accepted by other indigenous peoples or colonists? Second, do indigenous practices allow for the generation of sufficient surplus production to meet the "essential" needs of colonists or even other indigenous populations? And, three, are the resource management systems employed by indigenous peoples sustainable?

Gathering

Indigenous populations throughout the Americas all depend to some degree on the gathering of wild plants, animals and inorganic materials. Few researchers have studied the resource-gathering habits of the hundreds of groups that live in Latin American tropical rain forests. Taxonomic, pharmacological and nutritional data are limited. Few studies, for example, have identified wild foods that are gathered (see Cavalcante 1972, 1974); fewer still have have examined the nutritional content of these foods or the use and management of "wild" sources of food within overall management strategies of indigenous peoples. Most of the limited scientific work to date concentrates on the classification of wild plants and animals but excludes information about how each item is used (for example, see Williams 1960; National Academy of Sciences 1975 for an indication of the scope of the domesticated plant inventories of indigenous peoples; see also Berlin, Breedlove and Raven 1976 for Tzeltal Indians, Messer 1978 for Zapotecs, Lipp 1971 for Chinantec, Steggerda 1941 for the Yucatan Maya (all of Mexico); Duke 1975 for the Cuna of Panama; Hodge and Taylor 1975 for Island Caribs; Briston 1965 for the Sibundoy of Colombia; Prance and Prance 1972 for Brazil; and Berlin 1976 for the Aguaruna of Peru).

Posey estimates that the Kayapó Indians alone gather from some 250 species of plants for their fruits and hundreds of others for their nuts, tubers and leaves (1983a:883). In their 1983 survey, Posey and Anderson found that of 140 plants in the Kayapó area, "only two were not considered useful by the Kayapó. Equally astonishing is that the Kayapó claimed to have planted approximately 85 percent of the plants collected in ten sample forest 'islands'" (Anderson and Posey 1985).

A fair amount of data exist on materials that are used by indigenous groups in their villages — building materials (including the specific properties of timber and fibers), waxes, oils and ointments, ornaments, perfumes, pigments, dyes, gums and resins (e.g., Prance, Campbell and Nelson 1977). A closer examination of these plants could provide clues to the range of diversity in tropical rain forests as well as the impact of domestication and semidomestication on genetic structure.

Although half of the active ingredients of medicines encountered in an average drugstore originate in tropical rain forests, little is known about most of the medicinal plants used by indigenous peoples (see Poblete 1969; Krieg 1964). As Posey (1983a:883) writes,

> [M]edicinal plants . . . are regrettably overlooked due to the difficulty and expense of evaluating medicinal properties and a general disregard by Western science for folk medicine. Chemical and nutritional analyses exist for less than

one percent of the plants collected by Indians of Amazonia (Kerr, personal communication).

One topic in particular that has been overlooked is an inventory of the healing powers of various potions used by indigenous peoples to cure diseases endemic to the tropics. Little has been spent on examining the special disease and health problems of the populations of Latin American nations in general, or the populations that live in tropical rain forests in particular. Most of the research to date has focused on identifying materials that might prove useful in combating diseases in Western, industrialized countries.

Local individuals or groups who agree to help with surveys of flora and/or fauna rarely receive adequate financial remuneration—unlike the scientists who work in the area. Furthermore, even though indigenous groups might prove to be the best defenders of the genetic variability that the researchers are attempting to discover and eventually protect, few of the outsiders who collect materials and data from the local population assist the indigenous groups in defending their land rights.

Gathering often provides income for the rapidly increasing material needs of indigenous populations. Many indigenous groups have successfully collected and marketed rubber and Brazil nuts; other groups, unfortunately, are grossly exploited by colonists, local intermediaries or so-called patrons (see *Cultural Survival Newsletter* 4(3):7). Bunker reports that income generated from naturally occurring Brazil nuts compares favorably to income from an equivalent area of pasture (1981:56). More ecologically sustainable than pasture, Brazil nut collecting could create more long-term employment than pasture, as well.

Many indigenous groups depend on various insects or their products to provide a portion of their subsistence needs. A number of indigenous groups utilize such bee products as honey, wax, resin and pollen (Barrett 1925; Conzemius 1932; Metraux 1963; Chagnon 1978; and for the Kayapó Indian of Brazil, see Posey 1981, 1982b). Of the more traditional groups, only the Yanomamo Indians of Venezuela are reported to have attempted to market honey (Posey et al. 1984:97). Posey (1983a:888) reports that Kayapó lure certain species of bees to their fields because they associate their presence with increased crop yields.

Many indigenous groups eat ants, slugs and larvae of various beetles (Taylor 1975; Goldman 1963; Nimuendajú 1952; Posey 1978; Steward 1963; Steward and Metraux 1945). In fact there have been numerous reports (Chagnon 1968; Posey 1978, 1980) that sometimes the larvae of certain species of beetles are manipulated in a semi-domesticated manner so that they can be more easily utilized. Indians, knowing that adult beetles lay eggs on dead banana plants and old palm trees, bring the remains of these plants to villages,

Grubs, found in decaying tree trunks throughout Latin American rainforest areas, are gathered by indigenous peoples (above). Many groups bring tree trunks near to house or garden sites in order to attract beetles, which will lay eggs for grubs. Grubs are a rich source of protein (below).
©N.F. Whitten

fields and campsites in order to attract them. The adult beetles lay eggs which, after a period of time — depending on the particular species, region and season — develop into edible grubs. Denevan et al. (1984:353) report that the Bora of eastern Peru frequently visit old, fallow fields to collect grubs known to exist there. The article does not indicate whether Bora plant or retain certain species of trees in a conscious effort to encourage selected beetles to lay their eggs in the old fallows, or whether it is simply easier to get at beetles in old fallows than in naturally occurring forests.

The Kayapó of Brazil use a variety of leaf-cutting (*Azteca*) ants for a number of purposes. They establish ant colonies in mounds of newly cut plant material to speed the decomposition process. They also transport ants to garden sites in various parts of the forest because their strong odor appears to repel suava leaf-cutting ants (Posey n.d.:10).

Research into the useful products from specific wild plants as well as the conditions under which they grow could unearth the possibility that a number of wild species would be profitable for export production by local populations. Posey et al. (1984:97) suggest the following use for a natural resource.

> *Calathea lutea*, a tall herb that grows wild in swamps in the Amazon Basin, produces a wax similar to carbauba. This plant is easy to cultivate and harvest, and could provide jobs and income while exploiting otherwise unusable swampy areas in the region (National Academy of Sciences 1975:137-140).

Extractive Reserves in Western Brazil

In October 1985, rubber tappers from Brazil's western Amazonian states of Acre and Rondonia met to discuss new ways to protect Brazil's rain forests and the cultures they harbor. At the meeting the attendees drafted a proposal to create "extractive reserves," modeled on indigenous reserves, which would be set aside collectively for rubber tappers and/or indigenous peoples to manage. This proposal has been heralded as the first grassroots tropical forest conservation initiative to come out of Amazonia (Schwartzman 1986:41).

Rubber tappers arrived in the western Brazilian Amazon during the rubber boom between 1870 and 1910. After the boom died away, they stayed on and "supported themselves with mixed-crop agriculture, gathering, hunting, fishing and selling crude latex" (Schwartzman 1986:41). Schwartzman describes how the rubber tappers and the indigenous communities have overcome considerable differences and past conflicts to come together now in support of the idea of extractive reserves. The rubber tappers

> are the nucleus of a growing rural union movement in Acre and Amazonas. Many indigenous communities in this area also produce rubber for sale, and in both indigenous and Brazilian communities, producers' and consumers' cooperatives are emerging to eliminate exploitative middlemen.
>
> A long history of violence and mistrust exists among Indians and *seringueiros* [rubber tappers]. During the rubber boom, rubber barons organized *corridas* in Acre—seringueiros were sent on expeditions to massacre indigenous communities to drive them out. Many seringueiros still regard Indians on par with malaria, snakes and jaguars—dangers of life in the forest. But the seringueiros learned how to live in the forest from the Indians, and today the free seringueiro communities are economically similar to indigenous communities (1986:41).

Brazil's current constitution guarantees Indians rights to the land they occupy, but only about 30 percent of the lands thus far identified as "Indian" has even a minimal legal guarantee. A new constitution under review in Brazil would not guarantee the same level of land rights to Indians. Rubber tappers have no land rights under the old constitution or the new one awaiting ratification. The proposal for extractive reserves is intended to recognize and guarantee the rights of both groups to the lands that they now occupy and utilize.

During the past three decades, Indians and rubber tappers alike have seen the failure of many government colonization schemes in the Amazon. Not only have the poor and landless people brought into the region not benefited; in addition, they have displaced local populations who know how to make sustainable and productive use of forest resources. Through the establishment of designated extractive reserves and group rights to the use of the areas, both Indians and rubber tappers have a stake in the long-term economic productivity and sustainability of these areas.

The number of people involved in these activities is not insignificant. In 1980, more than half a million people made their living from extracting resources from the forests (for example, rubber, Brazil nuts, palm nuts and ipecac). The value of the materials collected in 1980 has been estimated at more than US$70 million (Schwartzman 1986:42).

Recently, the head of the Brazilian national miners union proposed an alliance whereby Indians and indigenist groups would support mining reserves and miners would support Indian reserves. Although such unilateral support may never happen, or may only occur in the distant future, some Indians have already forged agreements with groups of miners working in their areas. The Kayapó, for example, have made their own arrangements with independent miners who work on their reserves. As a result, the Kayapó now have more control over the miners' activities (in terms of their location and scope) and make more money from the mining activities than they did when the government's Indian organization was making the arrangements with individual miners or mining companies.

Research Priorities

1. Indigenous peoples are a largely ignored resource regarding rain forests; involve them directly in taxonomic research. Work with a wide variety of indigenous guides/assistants/informants, of both sexes, from groups living throughout tropical rain forests in Latin America to find out which resources these groups gather and what their primary characteristics and uses are. Information gained in this way could be useful in the search for improved foods, medicines and industrial materials.

2. Examine the impact of domestication and semi-domestication on the genetic structure of plants used by indigenous peoples. This might provide valuable insights into the domestication process itself.

3. Researchers should use information and knowledge of indigenous peoples to address the health, nutritional and economic problems of rainforest peoples in particular and Third World peoples in general.

4. Examine the long-term economic viability (including the value of local employment and the retention of rain forests) of gathering or mixed traditional management systems as compared to imported or peasant systems of agriculture currently being practiced or promoted in Latin American rain forests.

5. Examine the economic and pest control possibilities of indigenous uses of insects.

6. Discover items that are presently collected that have market potential. Such items could include nuts and roots, or plants whose seeds could be propagated and exported (such as various orchids or bromeliades). These latter items could be "double cropped" with avocado, cane, citrus trees, coffee, cocoa or even trees for lumber.

Hunting

Indigenous peoples throughout Latin American tropical rain forests depend upon hunted animals for a large portion of their food calories and, in many cases, for most of their protein. As a result they have an intimate understanding of the relationship between these animals and their environments. Many indigenous peoples exploit the juncture of different ecological zones (such as *varzea*, *cerrado*, swamps) within rain forests as the most productive hunting areas. They realize that greater numbers of animals often are found on the edges of different zones (on the Yekuana and Yanomamo, see Hames 1979:78,20). Other groups monitor the levels of game in various areas by examining the environment as well as the animals killed (e.g., on the Desana, see Reichel-Dolmatoff 1978:286). Thus, although traditional indigenous people have no fixed harvests, they develop over generations an ability to read clues from their environment, helping them to prevent the depletion of local species. With their intimate knowledge of animal behavior, indigenous hunters could serve as valuable consultants in such projects as planning conservation efforts and creating protected areas.

Naturally, the animals that are hunted in tropical rain forests are well adapted to their environment and are probably more resistant to local diseases than imported species. Meat from wild animals also provides "high protein-to-fat" ratios and resistance to diseases (de Voss 1977; Sternberg 1973; Surujbally 1977 in Posey et al. 1984:99). The efforts of traditional hunting groups to domesticate birds and other animals could provide useful information on species that might be promising for large-scale domestication or semi-domestication.

Indigenous people's knowledge about game animals could help to establish systems of protein generation, making wild animals an integral part of the food chain. For example, indigenous peoples — both contemporary and historical — in many areas of Latin American tropical rain forests already plant certain species of fruit and nut trees in their slash-and-burn gardens to extend the productivity of the plot *and* to attract wild pigs, paca, coati, deer, macaws, parrots and other animals that they traditionally hunt (see Carneiro 1960; Gross 1975:536; Ross 1978a:10; Posey 1982a; Linares 1976; Hames 1979). As Posey's research among the Kayapó demonstrates,

> The Kayapó are aware of the attractiveness of these abandoned garden sites to wildlife populations, and in dispersing their fields great distances from their villages maximize the area they can efficiently manage. This large scale management strategy produces forest reserves where game is attracted in artificially high densities, thereby improving the yields from hunting efforts (Posey et al. 1984:104).

Various authors (Goodland and Bookman 1977; Goodland, Irwin and Tillman 1978; Smith 1977; Vasey 1979) have proposed that game animals could be farmed in a form of "semi-domestication"; this could become one essential long-term strategy for development in tropical rain forests in Latin America. Such systems would improve the diets of indigenous groups and subsistence settlers who do not already practice this form of land management (Goodland 1980:17; Posey et al. 1984:99). Some of these game animal species might even be domesticated and raised in sufficient quantities for sale of surplus production. More research must be undertaken, however, to determine how much hunting of each species could take place without seriously threatening the rainforest game population.

In addition to the meat that various game species provide, some birds and small mammals are also recognized by indigenous populations, as well as by *caboclos* (immigrant peasant farmers in Brazil's Amazon), for their value as seed distributors. Through their droppings or food storage techniques, such animals spread the vegetation from one area to another (Parker 1983:185,189). Recognizing the importance of this activity, indigenous groups

Yanomamö woman in northern Brazil with peccary taken in the day's hunt. Game is normally divided among the hunting party. ©N. Chagnon

and caboclos often restrain themselves from overhunting certain species in order to maintain the delicate balance.

The activities of some indigenous peoples, however, do pose significant threats to animal populations (see Redford and Robinson 1985). New weapons and other imported technology (outboard motors, hunting dogs, headlamps, dynamite) now allow indigenous groups to kill more efficiently those animals preferred by hunters for their subsistence value, or, increasingly, for their cash value in local markets. Gross et al. (1979) state that the "extent of market participation is closely related to the difficulty of making a living through traditional means." Hames (1979) points out that the adoption of some of the trappings of modern civilization can cause or increase the overhunting of certain species.

Redford and Robinson (1985:43-44) write,

> It is clear from the preliminary results of our survey that indigenous people hunting just for subsistence are capable of hunting at nonsustainable rates. Within their own hunting methods lie the seeds of eventual resource extinction. Unlimited harvesting may jeopardize not only the survival of animal populations, but also the long-term survival of peoples engaged in such harvesting. Many investigators have shown that as people enter a market economy, they change their patterns of faunal use and concentrate more on commercially attractive species.

Nietschmann, for example, attributes changes in Miskito Indian hunting practices in Nicaragua to the depletion or extermination of hawksbill turtles, crocodiles, caiman, otters, spotted cats and lobsters. He also notes that as a result of the rapid adoption of commercial turtle hunting among the Miskito, "[s]ome Miskito are aware of the ecological blind alley they are entering by becoming dependent on declining resources. But, they have few alternatives which provide monetary return" (1972:66).

Although the adoption of modern weapons by indigenous peoples reduces the effort required to take game, it also increases their need for cash (to buy shells and so on) and their dependence on the cash economy. In some areas, indigenous peoples no longer know how to hunt with traditional weapons.

Some researchers do not believe indigenous people are the primary cause of declining game populations. Smith (1974:56) points out that the pressure on forest game species often comes from colonists who do not "respect forest and animal spirits" as indigenous societies do. AMARU IV remarks that "in Latin America as a whole indigenous subsistence hunting is almost negligible in comparison to commercial hunting" (1980:45) and that most commercial hunting is not done by indigenous peoples. Evidence to support this general conclusion, however, is not provided.

What is clear, however, is that with increasing populations and shrinking land bases, indigenous peoples throughout the Americas will have to discover alternative sources of protein if game species are not going to become depleted to the point of extinction. In the past, when the territory available to each tribe was larger, groups would simply move on to other areas of the forest where game was easier to capture. That is not possible today. Thus, most groups are attempting to obtain land rights which would fix their hunting territory, while at the same time they are exploring other avenues to increase their cash income and reduce their dependence upon hunting. Support for these efforts from those concerned about the preservation of biological diversity in fragile rainforest environments could help to insure the survival of the forests and all their inhabitants.

Research Priorities

1. Conduct investigations into the diversity and density of animals in rain forests with the aid of indigenous hunters, in order to determine areas or species that require protection.

2. Work with indigenous hunters to provide alternative sources of food and/or income to protect species that are endangered as a result of hunting or environmental degradation.

3. Work with indigenous populations to determine appropriate domestic species that could be substituted for endangered game species.

4. Determine which birds or other animals already exist in a semi-domesticated state; pinpoint those that might be promising for large-scale domestication.

5. Analyze the relationship of animal density in rain forests to the activities of indigenous peoples before such activities are curtailed under the guise of conservation.

6. Investigate the conservation principles and effects of hunting taboos.

Fishing and the Use of Aquatic Resources

Many researchers cite fishing – and other uses of aquatic resources – as one of the most promising forms of indigenous resource management, with potential for much larger-scale development efforts (see Goodland 1980:14). The indigenous populations of many tropical rain forests make use of a number of species of fish, mammals, reptiles and vegetation that live in the river systems of their areas or have a direct association with these systems. Amazonia, for example, contains the largest diversity of freshwater fish of any region in the world (Smith 1981:18); fish provide a substantial proportion of protein for most indigenous groups that live there (Ross 1978a; Sternberg 1973). Fish are better converters of food to protein (Ackefors and Rosen 1979, cited in Posey et al. 1984:101) than any other major protein source in Latin America; they provide local inhabitants with large quantities of essential amino acids (Bell and Canterbury 1976).

Some groups, both indigenous and caboclo, depend on the capture or trade of aquatic resources for most of their subsistence needs (Parker et al. 1983:193-198), particularly those groups that live in areas where regular flooding often limits agricultural production. As a result, such groups have developed an intimate understanding and vocabulary for describing the relationships of aquatic flora and fauna as well as the relationship of the aquatic systems to the surrounding flood plains. For the most part, the information crucial to their successful long-term subsistence strategies is scarce – information, for example, on the microsystems found at different depths of large and small rivers, at the mouths of large and small rivers, in flooded forests and temporary summer pools and data on the interaction of nonaquatic flora and fauna with the various microenvironments found in aquatic systems (Parker 1981:296).

Considerable commercial fishing, both on a large and small scale, takes place on rivers in rainforest areas, notably in Amazonia, but little research has been done on the major species taken or the impact of the fishing efforts (Smith 1981:121). According to Goulding, "commercial exploitation appears to be drastically reducing the population of these fishes" (1980:154, cited in Posey et al. 1984:99).

A number of game species have been semi-domesticated by indigenous peoples for some time. Turtles, for example, are efficient protein producers and, because they are considered a food delicacy internationally, could be a valuable export commodity (see Smith 1974:85; Sternberg 1973:258). In Amazonia, caiman, which can be bred in captivity (Montague 1981), pro-

Chiara Indians setting fish traps in the Amazon region in Brazil.   ©H. Schultz

vide meat for local consumption and hides for export; they also recycle nutrients that are essential for other flora and fauna (Fittkau 1973).

Some indigenous groups living along the the Xingu River in central Brazil have long used the water hyacinth to make salt. Recent studies show that the hyacinth can also purify sewage (one-third hectare purifies one ton per day) and filter out toxic heavy metals (Myers 1979:78). In addition, as cited in Posey et al. (1984:99),

> a variety of other water plants that form familiar "floating meadows" generate as much as seven tons of biomass per hectare per day (Myers 1979:78). These floating meadows provide food for numerous invertebrates which in turn are consumed by fish (Smith 1981:13).

Although detailed studies of Amazonian riverine systems are only now being undertaken (Goulding 1980; Smith 1981), initial reports suggest that development projects undertaken in some areas (for example, the clearing of the varzea forests for intensive agricultural use) have a negative impact on the plants and animals that live in adjacent waterways. For example, loss of varzea forests could decrease shade, increase water temperature and affect spawning and breeding. It could also change runoff and flooding patterns as well as overall water quality. Furthermore, many species of fish rely on fruit from trees growing on riverbanks or that which falls during seasonal flooding. Some fish spawn at the same time as flooding and fruiting occur.

As Posey et al. (1984) conclude,

> some aquatic faunal and floral species appear to present possibilities for surplus production within an integrated system of management. The potential for implementing aquatic management systems is an area requiring considerably more study. As Goulding (1980:254) points out, "... a better understanding of the natural fisheries and their proper management will be the best method for assuring a continual supply of fish to the Amazonian region for years to come." Those persons possessing the best understanding of the natural fisheries in Amazonia are the indigenous populations who have successfully exploited these resources for millenia.

Chernela (1982:17) is explicit about the relationship perceived by the Uanano Indians of Brazil between the fish that form the basis for their diet and the forest.

> The ideology of reciprocity sets behavioral norms and constraints. This is illustrated in the interplay of fishing beliefs and practices. The Uanano describe fish spawning as a fruit-exchange dance. Any interruption of these dances or interference in the supply of fruits requisite to them is severely punished by

Tukano fish trap in northwest Amazon.   ©J. Chernela retribution of the fish elders. While adult fish are caught as they swim back from the "dances," in exchange, the Uananos protect the offspring and preserve their food source — the forest. The Uanano depend upon the generosity of the fish and the forest and avoid offending them.

The Uanano relationship to both fish and forest appears to be largely responsible for the protection of their economic base, but it is doubtful that colonists would ever accept this same belief system.

Tukano Fishing—Brazil

A number of indigenous peoples have developed intricate systems of resource management that maintain a sustainable balance between harvest rates and yields of areas. For most of these peoples the resource management systems are deeply embedded in their cultures. Chernela (e.g. 1987a) has written extensively about a fascinating system of fish management employed by the Tukano Indians of the Uaupes basin in the northwest Amazon. The Tukano reserve the forested river margin for fish and fishing. Yet, as Chernela writes, "fishing may be restricted to as little as 38 percent of the total river margin available. The result is a management system which allows for, yet distinguishes, human use areas and animal refuge areas" (1987a:50).

For generations the Tukano Indians of the Upper Rio Negro have chosen to preserve the riparian forests rather than to deforest this area for agriculture. The Tukano believe that the long-term economic benefits from fish production in the standing flooded areas of the forest are greater than those to be acquired from the agricultural use of the same area.

The Tukano, who number about 10,000, depend primarily on root crop cultivation and fishing for their subsistence needs. "Manioc is the principal carbohydrate source and primary crop, comprising about 85 percent of garden yields. Apart from a few small mammals and birds, fish provide almost all animal protein" (Chernela 1987a:50).

The Uaupes basin releases little inorganic material to enrich the water. Thus, the Uaupes' waters are nutrient deficient. Not only do these waters not have the basic nutrients that form the basis of the food chain upon which fish depend, but their high content of acids and metals is actually deleterious to fish. Fish in such rivers derive their food from substances that fall into the river from the banks, or the food that is derived from forest areas adjacent to the river during two annual floods. At these times "the rivers swell and overflow their banks, merging the aquatic and terrestrial realms. Fish gorge themselves — spreading through the flooded forest and feeding on the abundance of forest foods only then available" (Chernela 1987a:50).

As fishermen dependent upon these river systems, the Tukano are aware of the relationship between their environment and the life cycles of fish, particularly the role played by the adjacent forest in providing nutrient sources that maintain vital fisheries. Strong Tukano proscriptions prohibit deforestation or cultivation of the river margin which is viewed as part of the aquatic system (1987a:50).

The Tukano believe that the forested riverbanks belong not to humans but to fish; therefore, they cannot be cut. Furthermore the soils on the riverbanks are as poor as those further inland, so there is no particular advantage to farming them. More food can be taken from the areas by letting the fish use them than by farming them.

Taboos are key to the Tukano system of sustainable resource management, and more fishing taboos abound during the flooding seasons than at any other time. Tukanoan taboos rest on two important concepts — boundedness and reciprocity. Tukano believe that distinct groups of humans and animals (in this case, fish) have proper places for sitting and breathing. Because the ancestors rest there and souls are recycled in alternate generations there, such locations should not be disturbed. Thus, the fish own the margins. Tukano also believe in reciprocity. In the case of fishing taboos, they believe that if fish are taken from restricted areas, the ancestors of the fish will take infant children — one child for one fish. Chernela (1987a) suggests that by examining the location of the guardian spirits and the associated taboos, we can begin to see their importance in sustaining the fish population.

Unlike most other researchers, Chernela has examined carefully the relationship between taboos and conservation of resources. Tukano taboos restrict fishing. In one village, five groups had dominion over various areas of the river that could be exploited (1987a:51). However, 26 guardian spirits restricted access to these potential fishing locations. One of the five groups (containing 38 people) in the village, for example, controlled fishing on 8.8 km of the Uaupes and 29 of its tributaries — a total of 164.8 km of river front. In this case, 17 of the 29 tributaries (62 percent of the lengths of all streams) were prohibited for fishing because of the presence of guardian spirits. These 17 areas are reported to be spawning areas for one of the most common fish sought after in the area. Such taboos work to conserve fish stocks.

Since the rising waters are associated with fish spawning runs, the correlation is clear: all potential spawning areas are restricted, either permanently or during spawning seasons. In the long run, the consequences of such proscriptions could prove critical to the maintenance of the fish populations.

Through the belief of spirit guardians, a nutrient-poor river system is managed in such a way that the possibility of irreversible damages to the resident fish populations is greatly reduced.

Traditional Tukanoan human-fish relations are governed by rules of balance and reciprocity. An object taken from one realm is compensated by an object taken from another. Neither man nor fish is the superior party; instead, each is of equal power to destroy. In contrast with Western belief models, for Tukano, boundaries are respected and reciprocity the mode of boundary-crossing. Breaching the rules creates imbalance and retaliation. The numbers of both humans and fish are seen as finite and precarious, locked into a carefully monitored exchange relationship (Chernela 1987a:52).

The Tukano have discovered that by maintaining forests and restricting fishing they can make a potentially sterile system relatively productive.

Today the Tukano are faced with problems resulting from Western beliefs about productivity in rainforest areas. These beliefs maintain that river margins (*varzeas* in Brazil) are the best — that is, least destructive — areas in tropical rain forests to use for agriculture. This belief stems from the notion that flooding replenishes the fertility of surrounding areas. In the case of black-water rivers, however, just the opposite occurs — the flooding, in fact, enriches the river.

Western beliefs are especially destructive to Tukano management belief systems because they contribute to the loss or abandonment of traditional information that young Tukano must learn to maintain the system. Younger Indians who leave the villages and attend boarding schools have little opportunity to learn from their elders. Furthermore, many of the teachers, albeit with good intentions, discourage their students from learning things that they consider backward or superstitious. To show how quickly these knowledge systems can be lost, Chernela reports that in 1979 elders named 26 fish guardians. In 1985, children from the same village attending a nearby school could name only a few.

Puerto Rastrojo Natural Resource Management—Colombia

In October 1986, Cultural Survival approved funding to permit local Indian involvement in the development and implementation of a conservation and management program to protect the endangered giant river turtle (*P. expansa*) in the Rio Caqueta area of the Colombian Amazon (Leon 1986:78-80). The project and the overall program functions under the auspices of the Fundacion Estacion de Biologia Puerto Rastrojo (FBPR), an applied biological research institute that has been performing biological, ecological and anthropological research in the Colombian Amazon for a number of years. Since 1983, the World Wildlife Fund has helped FBPR to undertake research and to establish a national park along the Caqueta River.

Despite existing protection laws, the giant river turtle, the largest freshwater turtle in the world, is a highly endangered species due to the overexploitation of its eggs and meat for commercial purposes. It has long been used by both Indians and mestizos throughout the Amazon, but the Caqueta River is practically the only major river in the Colombian Amazon where it still exists.

Using Indian assistants, researchers are now collecting information that will allow them to determine the history and current levels of turtle use in the area as well as its cultural significance to the Indians. Local Indians are also being trained to play an active role in the management program. The national park was created, at least in part, to protect the turtles' nesting areas.

The project is designed to integrate park and resource management into the Indians' traditional forms of social and political organization, and to reinforce existing Indian community resource management systems. This will increase the program's likelihood of acceptance by local Indian communities and their willingness to become involved in the long-term, sustainable management of the turtles.

The project is presently searching for ways in which Indians can benefit from the limited commercial exploitation of the turtle by eliminating the white intermediaries who currently monopolize such commercial activities. In addition, other income-generating activities must be developed in order to reduce the reliance on giant turtle trade.

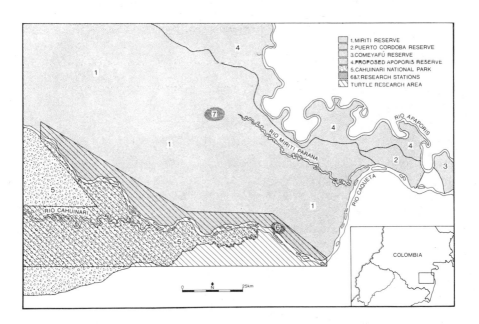

Fig. 1. Puerto Rastrojo resource management area, Colombia.

Research Priorities

1. What sustainable, commercial fishing potential exists in tropical rain forests? Which species are now being exploited? Are their stocks being depleted?

2. What species (for example, turtles or caiman) could be domesticated or semi-domesticated and provide significant sources of food or cash to local residents?

3. Determine if plants — such as the water hyacinth — can be used to purify sewage or filter toxic heavy metals from waters in the Third World or elsewhere. Which other rainforest, aquatic plants might have nutritional or economic uses?

4. What effect does deforestation have on aquatic life in rainforest areas?

5. What effect do major dams, such as those proposed in Brazil, have on aquatic life?

6. What effect does mining and the use of mercury have on aquatic life and the health of human populations downstream?

7. Do any indigenous groups in Latin America control rivers that go through or adjoin their land? What effect would this have on stemming deforestation and protecting aquatic resources?

Swidden Agriculture

The plants domesticated by indigenous peoples in Latin American tropical rain forests are largely overlooked as potential crops for consumption or industrial uses outside their traditional settings. Some of the aboriginal crops are well known (potato, sweet potato, manioc, yam, arrowroot, cashew, pineapple, peanut, chili pepper, papaya, squash, avocado, guava, lima and kidney beans, cacao and corn, to name but a few) and are now grown and depended on in many parts of the world; many others remain absolutely or relatively unknown, unutilized in Western agriculture. Another yield from traditional gardens, often overlooked, is the use of leaves for food: the leaves and/or flowers of sweet potato, pumpkin, squash, cassava and some beans are edible.

Many researchers conclude that the cultivars of indigenous peoples "demonstrate a great economic potential and lend themselves to large-scale exploitation" (National Academy of Sciences 1975; Williams 1960, as cited in Posey et al. 1984:101). The variety of crops grown by indigenous peoples could allow for considerable experimentation and adaptation of varieties to a number of different ecological zones.

Indigenous land-use patterns and management practices in Latin American tropical rain forests depend on those native plants which have a proven capacity to produce under local conditions (Alvim 1972, 1980; Lathrap 1970:37-38). A number of groups have adopted imported crops on a limited basis — if those crops produce under local conditions and do not disrupt the ecological diversity essential to minimizing the risk of crop failure. Like most cultivators, they experiment with new crops cautiously, gradually adopting those that prove successful themselves and abandoning those that do not.

Hecht asserts that crops domesticated by indigenous groups more efficiently utilize locally available nutrients than do imported cultivars from mid-latitude production systems (1981, personal communication, cited in Posey et al. 1984:101). This implies that local domesticates would not depend on fertilizers to the same extent as imported crop varieties.

A number of indigenous cultivars require more labor and give lower absolute yields than do imported varieties. Because indigenous cultivars are often high in secondary compounds (toxins, such as cassava) or are covered with spines (many fruits and squashes), food preparation is very labor intensive. However, these same characteristics often make such cultivars very pest resistant. A complex formula to evaluate the acceptability of indigenous cultivars for wider use would have to include information about growth, yields, preparation for consumption, labor requirements and impact on the

Mekranotí swidden plot cut and burned just prior to planting. Note that a number of trees have been lopped to allow for new growth. ©D. Werner

Mekranotí harvesting manioc in a swidden plot. As with many crops in rainforest areas, manioc is planted with cuttings from the previous crop, thus avoiding seed germination problems in the tropics. ©D. Werner

environment. Beliefs and values would ultimately determine the acceptability of choices of new cultivars based on any of these issues.

Although the adaptability of local varieties is an important factor in the success of indigenous production systems, the intimate knowledge of microenvironments by indigenous planters is equally important. This knowledge allows indigenous cultivators to place plants, even within small gardens, in the precise place — based on assessments of soil, shade, associated crops and drainage — where they will do best (Frechione 1981:55; Hames 1980b:20-21; Leeds 1961:19; Smole 1976:132-135).

Many indigenous cultivators have soil classification systems that are as sophisticated as those of Western scientists. Such groups recognize that gross distinctions in soil types are not a sufficient basis for evaluating the production potential of possible agricultural sites. Stevens, for example, writes,

> Systematic study of the soils of the Yucatan Peninsula, wherein the Postclassic Maya Area was situated, was begun by the Maya themselves. For the various kinds of soil they developed a specific nomenclature which survives in the present-day vernacular of Yucatecan agriculturalists. Ortis (1950) has found some of the Maya terms sufficiently compatible with modern procedures of soil classification that he adapted them as names of families and series within the Terra Rossa, Rendzina, and other intrazonal groups (1964:303).

Many indigenous groups planting slash-and-burn plots employ a number of different methods of planting, which include using seeds, seedlings and cuttings. In addition, they leave a number of plants in the plot or top them and allow them to regrow.

There is no need to overly romanticize indigenous cultivators, however. Some individual indigenous cultivators obviously have more skill at identifying relatively better garden sites or microenvironments for planting various kinds of crops than others. Some have been known to forget where they have planted seeds and needlessly replant the same area. However, the act of reading the environment and interpreting subtle clues about planting is common to all, and, for the most part, distinguishes indigenous farmers from the colonists in their areas.

Indigenous agricultural systems have been described as having "positive soil conservation effects" (Posey et al. 1984:101). These systems might be better described as having fewer harmful effects on the soil than other agricultural practices because they "minimize the time that soils are exposed to the destructive impact of direct sunlight and tropical rains" (Posey et al. 1984:101). Soil erosion and leaching, which are results of decreased sunlight and heavy rain damage, are reduced in indigenous gardens. Indigenous gardens more closely mimic the dense, multilayered forest canopy than do other farming practices that have been imported into rainforest areas.

Most indigenous peoples cultivate a large number of crops within a given garden plot. Some researchers have speculated that this great variety allows the groups to maintain an inventory of staple crops that can be used later on, when local environmental or climatic conditions change (Hames 1980b:20). Indigenous groups, however, because of their detailed environmental knowledge, do know which crops will do better in each soil type under different drainage conditions when interplanted with other crops in the same area.

A number of indigenous peoples utilize highly sophisticated planting techniques that enrich the soil and reduce the threat of insect pests. The methods used to plant peanuts by the Bora Indians of eastern Peru demonstrate some of these techniques.

> In a small area from which manioc has recently been harvested, soil (previously loosened by manioc growth and root decay) is gathered and packed into several dozen mounds measuring from 0.5 to 1 meter square. Ashes brought from home cooking fires are mixed in with soil as fertilizer. Between six and a dozen shelled peanuts, previously soaked overnight in an insecticide solution of crushed basil leaves and water to prevent ant predatoriness are planted in the mounds (Denevan et al. 1984:348).

Indigenous peoples utilize a number of dispersed garden sites to ensure

Mekranotí with ears of corn grown in a swidden plot.

©D. Werner

subsistence production and reduce the risk of total crop failure. Researchers have found that caboclos, too, realize that environmental changes (flooding or rainfall variations, for example) could wipe out all the crops planted in a single area; to prevent this, they plant crops in a number of different ecological zones (Parker et al. 1983:183). In some cases they plant most of their crops in less fertile but safe environments due to the calculated risks of planting only in the better but more easily flooded soils.

The utilization of small, intercropped, dispersed sites also reduces the threat of insect and disease damage to crops (Pimental, Levin and Olson 1978; Posey 1979; Stocks 1980). This in turn reduces the need for costly pesticides, which might endanger human populations as well as the environment and certainly increases the need for cash. Finally, the utilization of small dispersed garden sites throughout rainforest areas rather than larger clearcut fields allows the forest to incorporate the gardens more easily when they are left fallow.

Many indigenous groups clear their plots selectively, recognizing and saving species they find useful. As Denevan et al. (1984), write, "Valuable timber species, such as tropical cedar, are routinely spared during clearing, and various palms and other useful trees are commonly left in or on the edges of newly cleared fields; others may copice and be protected" (1984:347).

Some researchers have found that dispersed garden sites, in contrast to either more intensively utilized fields or untouched tropical rain forests, stimulate the growth of wildlife populations (Hames 1979; Linares 1976; Ross 1978), thus providing a greater abundance of game animals for hunting. As mentioned above, many historic and contemporary indigenous peoples in the Americas manipulate the wildlife population by producing an abundance of food crops which attract animals that, in turn, can be hunted. Other groups, such as the Bora, plant maize, which is used mainly to feed poultry (Denevan et al. 1984:349)—an indication that they not only have domesticated animals but are in a position to increase production (and income) when and if markets expand. Furthermore, by having corn, chickens and eggs, they have diversified their marketable produce.

Under conditions of limited or no population growth, dispersed garden sites are only a small part of the total surface area of the adjacent rain forests. For that reason, there is always a primary forest reserve that can serve as a ecological reserve for plant and animal species in the region (Gomez-Pompa et al. 1982; Lovejoy and Schubert 1980). As Posey et al. note, "Therefore, species are not only protected from extinction but are reserved close at hand for re-establishment in the 'abandoned fields'" (1984:102).

Studies of indigenous systems of shifting cultivation, under conditions of stable populations, show them to be extremely productive per unit of labor utilized (Carneiro 1961:53; Harris 1972:247) and per unit of land cultivated (Carneiro 1961:52-53). Smole, for example, found that the Barafiri

Yanomamo could produce 23.16 tons of plantain per hectare, which converts to 15.6 million calories per hectare (1976:150). Frechione's study of the Yekuana of southern Venezuela shows that they have produced as much as 30 tons of manioc per hectare, which yields 23.8 million calories from the raw tubers and about 6 million calories per hectare from processed manioc plants (1981:101).

Shifting cultivation, however, requires an area of land that is much larger than that being cultivated — probably at least 20 times larger — to ensure the maintenance of soil fertility through the proper length of fallow. Factors that can reduce productivity from shifting cultivation are natural increases in the local population, immigration of others into an area or expanded cultivation of cash crops with the same land base.

Most slash-and-burn garden sites in Latin American tropical rain forests are assumed to produce crops for periods of only two to five years. In reality, the crops that are taken in the first years are only a part — sometimes not even accounting for most production — of a given site (Alcorn 1981; Denevan et al. 1984; Carneiro 1961). Posey points out that "abandoned" fields

> continue to bear produce for many years; e.g., sweet potatoes for four to five years, yams and taro for five to six years, manioc for four to six years, and papaya for five or more years. Some banana varieties continue to bear fruit for 15 to 20 years, urucu (Bixa orellana) for 25 years and cupa (Cissus gongylodes) for 40 years (Posey n.d.:11-12).

Denevan et al. write that the most productive stage of the fallow is from four to 12 years although harvesting of some species continues "20 to 30 or more years" (1984:354). In addition to lengthening the productive cycle of slash-and-burn agriculture, the different types of fruit trees that are planted by the Bora ensure yields throughout the year, providing food not only for the Bora but also for animals that they hunt.

Many researchers have pointed out the continued use of so-called abandoned sites (see Denevan 1971:508-509 for the Campa in eastern Peru; Posey 1982, 1983a, 1984a for the Kayapó in central Brazil; Basso 1973:34-35 for the Kalapalo in central Brazil; Eden 1980 for the Andoke and Witoto in the Colombian Amazon; Smole 1976:152-156 and Harris 1971:487,489 for the Yanomamo of Venezuela; Espinoza 1980 for the Shuar of eastern Ecuador; Hames 1980:9 for the Yanomamo and Yekuana of Venezuela; and Bergmann 1974:147-148). Few studies, however, have thoroughly examined this form of land use and management.

Some researchers have assumed that indigenous cultivators return to "abandoned" fields for residual crops from periods of intensive cultivation. But, as Denevan et al. write,

> indications are that actual management occurs, including planting and protec-

tion as well as utilization of certain useful wild plants that appear at various stages of fallow succession....

....For the Bora [of eastern Peru] there is no clear transition between swidden and fallow, but rather a continuum from a swidden dominated by cultivated plants to an old fallow composed entirely of natural vegetation. Thirty-five years or more may be required before the latter condition prevails. Abandonment is not a moment in time but rather a process over time (1984:346,347).

Although "abandoned" garden sites continue to provide sources of food for indigenous peoples, they are rarely included in the calculations of the productivity of slash-and-burn agriculture made by Western-trained scientists. In addition to planted crops that produce after a garden site is abandoned, a number of wild plants that are part of the forest regeneration process are utilized by indigenous peoples (Denevan et al. 1982; Posey 1982a; Yde 1965:28,54).

In the past, many analysts assumed that slash-and-burn temporary garden sites produced high yields primarily because the areas cultivated were quite small. If, the analysts reasoned, the areas under cultivation were expanded to produce sufficient quantities for marketing, total production would decline — as in monocrop experiments in tropical rain forests. However, an increasingly large body of literature is drawing those assumptions into question (Carneiro 1961; Allen and Tizon 1973; Kloos 1971:38-39; Smole 1976:192-193). Some researchers have even asserted that dispersed gardens that are planted with a single, indigenous cultigen may be no more harmful to the environment than polycultural gardens (Frechione 1981:102-105; Harris 1971).

The Lacandon Maya, a rapidly disappearing Indian group living in Chiapas, Mexico's rain forest, have long practiced agroforestry in order to extend the life of slash-and-burn garden plots. Like many indigenous groups, the Lacandones practice a multilayered cropping system that replicates the tropical rainforest canopy. Nations and Nigh (1980) report that the Lacandones utilize up to 75 crop species on single-hectare plots.

After five to seven consecutive years of harvests in the same rain forest clearings, Lacandon farmers plant the plots with tree crops such as rubber, cacao, citrus and avocado. Far from being abandoned fields, these "planted tree gardens," as the Lacandones call them, continue to provide food and raw materials as the clearings regenerate with natural forest species (Nations and Komer 1983:235).

Nations and Komer claim that under such a system the "traditional Lacandon cultivator clears fewer than 10 hectares of rain forest during his entire agricultural career" (1983:235-236). The Lacandon system, extended into other rainforest areas, might serve as a model for rainforest exploitation that would

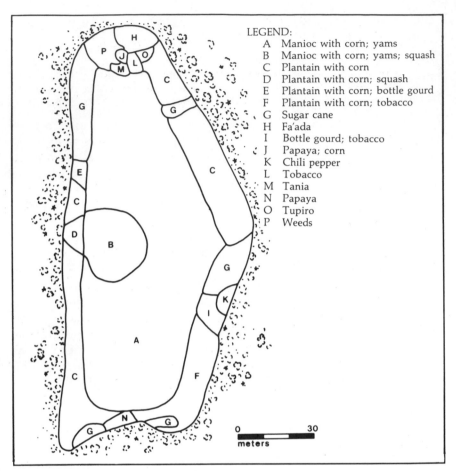

LEGEND:
A   Manioc with corn; yams
B   Manioc with corn; yams; squash
C   Plantain with corn
D   Plantain with corn; squash
E   Plantain with corn; bottle gourd
F   Plantain with corn; tobacco
G   Sugar cane
H   Fa'ada
I   Bottle gourd; tobacco
J   Papaya; corn
K   Chili pepper
L   Tobacco
M   Tania
N   Papaya
O   Tupiro
P   Weeds

Fig. 2. Planting patterns in a typical Yekuana garden, Venezuela.
(Source: Parker et al. 1983:182)

improve the quality of life of recently arrived colonists and simultaneously prevent the destruction of tropical rain forests.

Alternatively, a number of indigenous cultivators have both fields which are monocropped with staples as well as ones polycropped with many useful plants (Denevan et al. 1984:349). Crop composition in each field appears to be determined, to a great extent, by the composition of crops that indigenous cultivators have or anticipate having in other dispersed fields. As Denevan et al. note, "Since a Bora family may have six or more fields of different ages and crop mixtures, diversity between the fields fulfills the same function of assuring a supply of varied crops as does diversity within a single field" (1984:349).

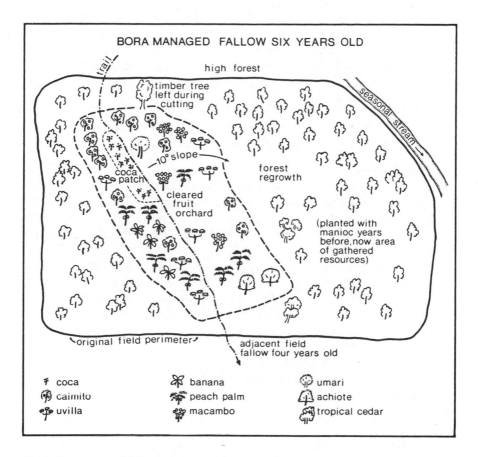

Fig. 3. Bora-managed fallow, six years old.
(Source: Tracey 1982:16)

Although indigenous peoples living in tropical rain forests can produce surpluses and, for the most part, would be happy to earn income from them, there is little economic incentive for them to do so (Allen and Tizon 1973; Carneiro 1961:54; Nimuendajú 1974:115-116). Most of these groups live in regions of such low population density that little marketing infrastructure exists in their area; they spend more to get food crops to the market than they receive for them. The development priorities of many Latin American countries will have to shift before the marketing of indigenous food crops will become widespread. Food crops, rather than export crops, will need to become priorities. Relatively low returns over a long period of time will have to be accepted; slightly larger short-term returns quickly lead to degradation of the environment and little or no production in the near future.

Those items for which a market exists, even when cash returns are minimal, are often produced by indigenous peoples. Logs, for example, can be floated downriver. The planting of valuable tree species such as tropical cedar, by such groups as the Bora, not only reflects their marketing orientation but their willingness to invest in crops that will not be harvestable before their children are grown (Denevan et al. 1984:355).

Shifting Cultivation and Agroforestry

Although shifting cultivation has been discounted as a possible focus of development in Latin America's rain forests (Goodland 1980:14-15), a number of researchers believe that it can serve as the basis for ecologically sustainable and economically viable systems of agricultural production (Posey et al. 1984:103; Dickinson 1972; Janzen 1973; Sioli 1980:266-269) and agroforestry (Denevan et al. 1982).

Global reviews of agroforestry systems — production that combines tree crops, cash crops, food crops and animals, or some combination of these — include research by Combe and Budowski (1979), Nair (1982) and Lundgren and Raintree (1983). Reviews of agroforestry systems in use in Central and South America include those by Budowski (1981), Hecht (1982), Salas (1979), Hart (1980) and Spurgeon (1980).

Agroforestry research, for the most part, has been conducted at disciplined or commodity-specific research institutes throughout the tropics. As Lundgren and Raintree (1983:9) point out,

There is, however, little ongoing research towards developing technologies and systems which, through the optimum use of multipurpose trees and shrubs address the multiple problems faced by small- and mediumsized subsistence (or mixed subsistence/cash) farmers or pastoralists in the tropics. This is where the great challenge and potential of agroforestry technology-generating research lies and where scope exists for almost unlimited innovative and imaginative thinking and work.

Likewise, a major recommendation of a recent report on tropical development by the US National Research Council (1982:4,5,146) encouraged research on traditional agroforestry systems of indigenous people before such knowledge is lost.

Clearly, not all swidden agriculture practices undertaken by indigenous peoples are for the ecologically sound reasons that they exhibit to outside observers. For example, more labor is required to cut larger slash-and-burn plots and only a limited market exists, at best, for surplus. The planting of tree crops to extend production in the face of encroaching forest may "solve

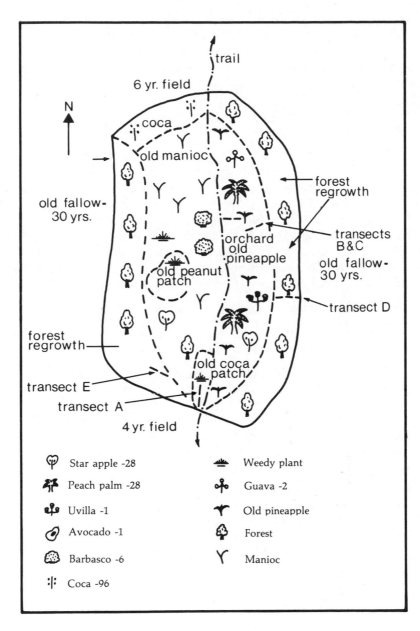

Fig. 4. Diagram of five-year-old transitional agricultural plot/fruit orchard of Bora Indians, Peru. (Source: Denevan et al. 1984:349)

a shifting cultivator's dilemma of how to maintain field production in the twilight of the cropping cycle..." (Denevan et al. 1984:349). It is not clear, furthermore, if indigenous cultivators would always clear small slash-and-burn plots if they had access to tools to clearcut larger areas and guaranteed markets.

Floodplain and River-Bottom
Drained Fields—Venezuela

Various Carib Indian groups living in Venezuela practiced annual agriculture on parts of stream beds and seasonally flooded plains next to rivers. In higher savanna areas Indians cultivated "only limited strips along the middle courses of streams" (Denevan and Schwerin 1978:23), which were suitable for unmodified swidden cultivation (Leeds 1961:14-15).

The Caribs also learned the technique of using ditches to drain saturated, swampy soils. Such activities were present in prehistorical sites — they were first reported in 1600 — but it is not known how long this agricultural technique was practiced in the area (Denevan and Schwerin 1978:23).

> Although there are hints that the Carib had occupied most of the eastern plains at the time of European discovery, there is no incontrovertible evidence of their widespread presence until the beginning of the seventeenth century.... It was mastery of the technique of draining the morichal swamps which border these rivers which made possible an adaptation to the particular conditions of the Mesas and facilitated widespread occupation of the area. This system of cultivation is clearly more intensive, in terms of both cropping frequency and labor inputs, than swidden or annual floodplain agriculture. Once perfected, it has changed little down to the present (Denevan and Schwerin 1978:23-24).

Denevan and Schwerin (1978:24) proceed to describe a series of ditched fields at Cachama which are "particularly numerous, large and complex, and they are the main means of cultivation by the community."

> In reclaiming a moriche palm swamp, sites are chosen where flooding is not excessive, where there is tall vegetation and hence better soil, and where leaf cutter ants are minimal. The first and most important task in preparing a field is the digging of ... ditches to provide adequate drainage for the plot.... This is difficult and strenuous due both to the wetness of the soil and the density of the undergrowth.... Ditches are made by cutting down through the grass sod with a machete. Then the earth is thrown out by hand or with a shovel. Most of the ditches are .3 to .7 m deep, .7 to 1 m wide and 10 to 100 m long, with spacing 10 to 20 m apart.
> Initially one or several large canals are excavated ... through a section. The largest ... follows a natural channel and drains into the Rio Cachama (see figure); it is 1.3 to 1.7 m wide and 1 to 1.3 m deep, and the maintained portions about one half km long. It is kept meticulously clean, and at the height of the dry season it was observed full of fast flowing water that had seeped

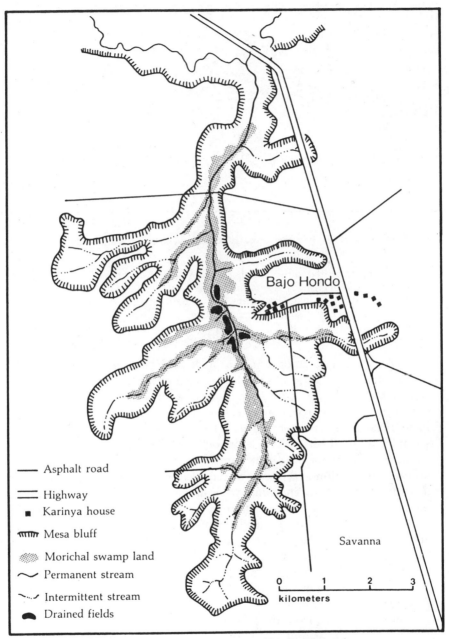

Bajo Hondo

— Asphalt road
═ Highway
■ Karinya house
ᴧᴧᴧᴧ Mesa bluff
░ Morichal swamp land
∼ Permanent stream
∼··✓ Intermittent stream
◗ Drained fields

Savanna

0   1   2   3
kilometers

Fig. 5. Map of the Río Cachama drainage basin, Bajo Hondo, Venezuela.
(Source: Denevan and Schwerin 1980:8)

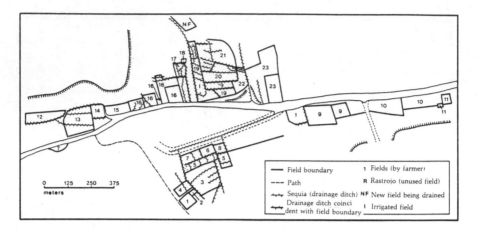

Fig. 6. Map of Bajo Hondo *morichal* fields, Cachama, Venezuela. Fields are numbered by owner. (Source: Denevan and Schwerin 1980:30)

in from the saturated subsoil. Other shallow tributary channels of the Rio Cachama are kept clean of vegetation and silt and serve as additional [canals]. After substantial drainage by means of the main ditches or improved channels, smaller ditches are dug around each field, and often very shallow ditches are dug across fields as well. . . . Complete drainage of a new or long abandoned section usually takes several years (Denevan and Schwerin 1978:24-25).

Groups of half a dozen or so men provide the labor required to undertake such construction. Labor is either exchanged or hired.

Once the fields are drained and somewhat dried out, clearing the undergrowth and the trees is much easier. After it is dry, all debris is burned. The moriche palm, however, is always left; its fruits supplement the diet and its fronds are used for making hammocks and roofs.

Manioc is the major crop grown in the fields; bananas are second in importance. Production and planting occur year round. At least half a dozen other tubers are grown (including yams and sweet potatoes) in addition to a number of more seasonal, seed crops (corn, carrots, beans, squash and gourds). The seed crops are normally planted at the onset of the rainy season, but the plots usually have enough moisture so that a second crop can be planted in the dry season (Denevan and Schwerin 1978:26).

Once the fields are drained and cleared they do not require much more labor to maintain than those plots cleared from heavy forests and only cultivated for two or three years. The fields must be weeded every two to three months. Weeds from the plots or the ditches are often spread on the ground of the plots as mulch. Not only does this improve soil fertility, but it also preserves moisture during the dry season. "Two to five hours every other day is adequate to keep the weeds under control, harvest the crops as they mature, and replant recently harvested sections" (Denevan and Schwerin 1978:28). Once harvests are completed, pigs are allowed to root for the remaining tubers.

Ditches are cleaned each year before planting. If the weeds get out of control, a communal work party may have to be called before the next crop can be planted, or fallowing may occur.

> The ecological reasons for fallowing are not completely clear, but excessive grass and weed invasion seems more important than fertility decline. During fallow, brush is allowed to grow up to two or three m before being cut and burned. Fields may also be long fallowed if they become excessively dry, or if buried by a thick layer of sand left behind by high water. Within a few years after abandonment the ditches become choked with silt and weeds and drainage deteriorates again. Groves of mangos are often planted during long fallowing (Denevan and Schwerin 1978:28).

Farmers reported that fields were usually cultivated for two to four years before being fallowed for one or two years, but some individuals reportedly cultivate the same fields for 20 years or more. Likewise, some fields might lie fallow for as long as 40 years. Most fields, however, are eventually reclaimed. The Cachama, for example, have occupied the same general site for more than 380 years. Their cultivation of less than 0.4 hectares of morichal drained fields (not counting house gardens) per household (six to eight people) indicates highly productive agriculture. By the late 1970s, the Indians' traditional agriculture had continued to survive in spite of a nearby major highway, employment opportunities in local oil industries and nearby towns and the efforts of the Ministry of Agriculture to encourage cultivation of upland savannas.

Conucos—Upper Orinoco, Venezuela

Bananas and manioc are the principal crops grown in the *conucos*, the swidden gardens of the Waika Indians of Venezuela. "These starch-rich staples provide the basic food supply of the Amerindians, who supplement it with protein obtained principally from terrestrial mammals, river fish and birds" (Harris 1971:478). In the past, these crops were grown in the swidden conucos in association with numerous other crops of secondary importance. The author notes that as Indians come into contact with outsiders and outside markets they tend to grow single crops (manioc, corn or even bananas) in some swidden plots.

In 1968, a Waika village, estimated at 150 to 200 people, cultivated about six hectares of swidden plots. The nine separate plots had been cleared in the previous dry season (December and January) and burned in early

February. Crops were planted in association, although either manioc, corn or bananas dominated. Even in this relatively isolated and traditional village, the main crops in the plots are intended to provide surpluses to be sold in the markets of nearby towns. Papaya and perennial cotton provided the upper canopy, and an aroid of American origin similar to taro, along with yams, arrowroot, manioc, bottle gourd, sugarcane, Indian arrowleaf and tobacco under the taller plants. All plants were propagated with cuttings; seeds were not used.

The positioning of plants in the conuco followed no regular plan but was guided by the necessity of avoiding tree stumps, felled trunks and forest debris that remained after clearance and burning. The effect of this apparently haphazard pattern of cultivation was to leave little bare soil exposed to the direct effects of insulation and raindrop impact, even in April soon after the annual weeding which the Waika conucos receive in March. The interplanting of species with different growth habits and root systems — trees, shrubs, and herbs, climbing and sprawling plants, root and fruit crops — also ensures effective vertical and lateral exploitation of available light, warmth, moisture and nutrients. In other words, by substituting a diverse assemblage of cultivated plants for the wild species of the forest this type of polycultural conuco simulates much more closely than monocultural plots do the structure and dynamics of the natural forest ecosystem. Indeed as the conuco ages its complexity is increased by the regener-

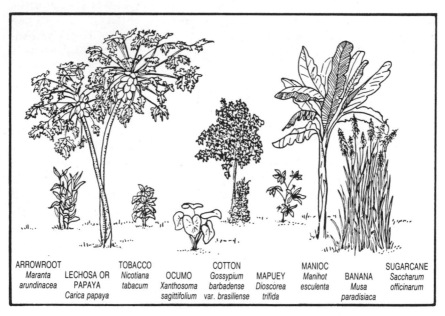

| ARROWROOT | | TOBACCO | | COTTON | | MANIOC | | SUGARCANE |
| Maranta arundinacea | LECHOSA OR PAPAYA Carica papaya | Nicotiana tabacum | OCUMO Xanthosoma sagittifolium | Gossypium barbadense var. brasiliense | MAPUEY Dioscorea trifida | Manihot esculenta | BANANA Musa paradisiaca | Saccharum officinarum |

Fig. 7. Schematic profile of a polycultural conuco, based on a Waika swidden plot near Ocamo, Venezuela.

ation of trees and shrubs not completely killed at clearance, as well as by the invasion of pioneer species from the margins of the surrounding forest (Harris 1971:480-481).

Conucos are normally cultivated for five or six years. As weeding and reclearing become more difficult, the plots begin to be used as secondary forests. In multicrop conucos, the transition to secondary forests is gradual, with harvests tapering off over a longer period of time.

Harris suggests a number of conclusions that can be drawn from the monocultural and polycultural conucos in the Upper Orinoco of Venezuela. Polycultural plots are cultivated for longer periods of time; those who cultivate them, therefore, are more stable and less mobile than those who cultivate monocultural plots. Weed invasion and forest regeneration appear to be the main cause of the abandonment of polycultural plots; with monocultural plots, declining fertility appears to be relatively more important. Banana production, for example, only begins to fall after about the fifth year. According to Harris, "forest gathering from abandoned polycultural swiddens has seldom been commented on in the literature on shifting cultivation, though it increases significantly the overall productivity of the system, at least in the Upper Orinoco" (1971:482).

Market-Oriented Agroforestry—Tamshiyacu, Peru

Padoch et al. (1985) have noted that most research undertaken on traditional swidden-fallow or agroforestry systems of resource management practiced in Latin America has been with tribal groups. The researchers note that such groups are relatively remote and not actively involved in market trade. Some mestizo peasant agriculturalists, however, practice cyclic agroforestry systems as a way to obtain significant cash income. Padoch et al. (1985:48) insist that the resource management practices of such groups, who are in large part dependent on the market economy, have not been adequately examined.

> The limitation of these studies to isolated, tribal communities has unfortunately suggested that such methods of resource use are known only to the most traditional groups and are suited merely for the production of their subsistence needs; as such, these systems would be of little utility as models for agricultural development. More recent investigations carried out by a number of independent researchers, however, indicate that similar systems can indeed be important cash producers (1985:48).

Mestizo producers in Tamshiyacu, 30 km southwest of Iquitos, Peru, on the Amazon River, "engage in a large number of agricultural and extractive activities, exploiting the varied land and water resources available to them" (Padoch et al. 1985:48). Hiraoka (1982) examined the income-generating and subsistence activities of the villagers. The resource use and management techniques he found

include the farming of upland sites under both high forest and fallow growth of varying ages, the cultivation of seasonally inundated low-lying sites, as well as fishing, hunting, and the extraction of a variety of forest products. The fields and forests of Tamshiyacu yield foods, fibres, handicraft materials, charcoal, and numerous other items which appear in both an active local market and the urban market in Iquitos (Padoch et al. 1985:49).

Subsequent research in the village indicated that production and prices varied greatly throughout the year and that monetary income in village households

is derived from a variety of activities and households differ greatly in the activities from which they derive the major portion of their income. (A more thorough study would probably have shown that an even wider array of income sources including fishing, small vegetable farming, and livestock production are important on a community-wide basis.) (Padoch et al. 1985:50)

As Table 1 indicates, slash-and-burn agroforestry fields not only supply most of the subsistence needs of the villagers, but most of their income as well.

Table 1
Major Sources of Income in Tamshiyacu

	Percent of annual income	
	Average	Range
Cultivated fruits	63	0-100
Intensively managed crops	21	0-65
Animal products	9	0-86
Charcoal	3	0-37
Forest fibers, handicrafts	2	0-17
Forest fruits, palm heart	1	0-13
Medicinal plants	0.5	0-7

(Source: Padoch et al. 1985:50)

According to the research, the slash-and-burn plots yield commercially valuable commodities for as long as 25 years. Crops change throughout the life of the field, but the commercial yields from the plots, in volume at least, are not insignificant (see Table 2). The information presented is estimated production for cash crops grown on a one-hectare plot after a six- or seven-year fallow. Most income is generated by fruits in the plots.

Table 2
Estimate of Commercial Production on One Hectare of Land

Year of land use Annual production (Major commercial products)	1	2	3	4	5	6	7	8-11	12-20	21-24	25
Charcoal (15-kg sacks)	500										600
Manioc (50-kg sacks)	60	5									
Pineapple (fruits, 100's)	5	15	15	30							
Plantains (20-kg racimes)	10	5									
Cocona (30-kg sacks)	5	5									
Cashew (fruits, 100's)	50	50	4								
Uvilla (1.5-kg bunches)		250	1000	100	5						
Peach palm (8-kg racimes)			60	120	80	40	40	40			
Umari (fruits, 100's)				100	200	300	400	600	600	400	
Brazil nuts (fruits, 100's)									5	5	

(Source: Padoch et al. 1985:53)

Padoch et al. describe a generalized cycle of land use and income generation from an average family's plot.

> The cycle is initiated when the standing vegetation in an area is cut. Then, if the vegetation was secondary forest, rather than burning all the slash in the manner typical of shifting cultivators, the larger woody vegetation is converted by Tamshiyaquinos to charcoal and sold in the market. Following clearing, the field is planted to a variety of annual and semi-perennial crops. . . . In the second year some of these crops are replanted and a number of perennials, most of them tree crops, are planted. After the initial period of two to five years, annual crop production is gradually phased out and perennial tree crops become the most important income producers from the plot. Such production can often continue for approximately 25 to up to 50 years if care is taken to maintain the fields and to protect them from the depredations of invading cattle. Cleaning of the plot, done several times a year while annuals and semi-perennials predominate, is gradually reduced in frequency to once or perhaps twice a year, just before umari, the most important crop, is to be harvested. As soon as production begins to fall significantly, anytime between the twenty-fifth and fiftieth year, the larger vegetation — mostly umari and Brazil nut trees — is cut and converted to charcoal. Following this second round of charcoal making, the field is generally fallowed for six years or so, during which time secondary growth invades the plot and, according to local farmers, begins to restore it so another production cycle can begin (1985:51-52).

The above description applies only to those plots that are most intensively used over long periods of time. It appears that many cultivators have additional plots in which charcoal is not made when the plot is initially cut or "fruit orchards" are never planted and fields are abandoned after only a few years of use (Padoch et al. 1985:52).

Villagers also indicate a number of other sources of products from the fields. "Forest fruits," either spontaneously generated or planted, account for a field's total production; given that the reuse of fallowed fields is common, it is likely that the density of "naturally" occurring fruit trees increases over time.

Animal products — both meat and skins — generate income for many families and "in some cases these materials may also be regarded as products of agroforestry fields. . . . When fruits are ripe, hunters will frequently build platforms near older fruit trees and watch for animals coming to feed" (Padoch et al. 1985:54).

Farmers in the village obtain income from a variety of sources; of the seven sources identified, however, five are wholly or partially from the slash-and-burn fields. Because fields have different production foci over time and because farmers keep a number of fields in various stages of production, farmers can sell a variety of products. "This strategy limits the risks inherent in specialization, spaces out the need for often scarce labor, and assures the households of some cash flow throughout the year" (Padoch et al. 1985:54).

According to the (unfortunately limited) surveys undertaken thus far with the villagers, not only does this type of resource management provide them with steady income,

> it also allows many of them to enjoy some of the highest average annual incomes to be found among rural dwellers of the region. . . . We estimated that some Tamshiyacu households obtained gross yearly incomes of close to US$5,000. although the mean for village households was a much more modest but still above average income of about US$1,200 (Padoch et al. 1985:55).

The authors are quick to point out that the system of resource management employed by village residents developed from techniques utilized by various tribal groups indigenous to the Amazon. The system, however, differs from tribal systems in a number of ways that present important implications for further research.

> Notably, some of the vegetation that is normally "slashed and burned" is . . . converted to charcoal and removed. Cleaning of the plot is continued for a longer period of time than appears to be typical among the traditional tribal groups previously described, and the creation and maintenance of an almost pure stand of umari and Brazil nut trees during most of the use cycle contrasts with the very complex older swidden-fallow fields [by traditional indigenous cultivators]. Most notable, however, is the commercial orientation of the system and the large cash returns households realize from sales of the products. Amazo-

nian cyclic agroforestry systems are obviously capable of being commercially successful enterprises, in addition to serving as sources of local household needs (Padoch et al. 1985:56-57).

As with most traditional or modified traditional resource management systems, a number of questions remain about the sustainability of this system. Briefly: how much land is required per family to maintain the present level of market integration? How much more land would be needed if the level of income was to increase—say to double? Is the system described above sustainable over the long term? What effect does it have on soil fertility? Could any types of technologies be introduced into the system that would increase its overall profitability without unduly jeopardizing the producers? Could profitability of the system increase, while production remains constant, by assisting producers to market produce when or where its value is higher by reducing the role of intermediaries or by increasing local storage capacity? Could such a system accept the introduction of nonperishables, which would increase its cash return to villages located farther away from large markets? Finally, to what extent does such a system depend on guaranteed land rights or titles? Would insecure land rights affect such systems as operated by either peasants or indigenous peoples?

Research Priorities

1. Which plants domesticated by indigenous peoples have nutritional or industrial uses outside their traditional settings?

2. A number of indigenous peoples are experimenting, on an ongoing basis, with imported crops. Instead of conducting ideal field trials with such crops, why not find out how they perform, under which conditions, in traditional plots? This will not eliminate the need for "scientific" field trials, but could indicate which trials might be more promising.

3. What ecological limits exist for traditional slash-and-burn systems of land use, either by indigenous peoples or peasants? What variables can be identified to predict environmental deterioration, sustainable resource use or loss of genetic resources? How would such indicators vary from one area to another?

4. Which indigenous forms of pest control might have wider application as alternatives to the use of pesticides?

5. Which methods of extending production in swidden fields might provide increased income to indigenous peasant cultivators in rainforest areas?

6. And, perhaps most important of all research topics, what is the relationship of insecure land rights — for either indigenous peoples or peasants — to environmental degradation?

Permanent Agriculture

Various systems of permanent or near-permanent agriculture have been practiced throughout the tropical rainforest areas of the Americas. Vast Indian populations in the Amazon undertook permanent cultivation of the seasonally inundated banks of the Amazon. Although these populations were decimated by their contact with European explorers, missionaries and colonists, today their successors (Indians, mestizos, caboclos and *riberenos*) continue to practice various combinations of permanent agriculture, shifting cultivation and agroforestry that are based on systems of sustainable resource management practiced in the region for centuries. Likewise, Mayans of Central America practiced permanent cultivation of raised fields throughout the area.

Research is now being undertaken on a number of permanent production systems — "orchard gardens," ridged fields, terraces and upgraded models of traditional slash-and-burn agroforestry and chinampa systems (Gordon 1969; Romanini 1978; Janka 1981; FAO/CHDF 1980; Nova and Posner 1980; Wilken 1977; Michaelson 1980; Denevan 1970; Parsons and Denevan 1967). These ecologically sensitive, intensive production systems offer alternatives to the imposition of monocropping systems, which are often introduced by colonists and planners in tropical rain forests.

Archeological evidence also sheds light on the economic activities of previous occupants of Central and South America's tropical rain forests (Siemens and Puleston 1972; Turner 1974; Adams 1982; Donkin 1979; Hammond 1977). The Maya of Central America, for example, "sustained huge populations in areas that, today, are being devastated by the agricultural practices of the modern world" (Nations and Komer 1983:236).

Linares' archeological research, for example, demonstrated that pre-Colombian occupants in Panama obtained food from house gardens as well as cultivated plots. These foods were supplemented, in turn, by the seasonal hunting of "wild" animals that were attracted to the crops.

Tropical rain forests may never support the same population densities as other areas; in the past, however, many areas are estimated to have supported populations 10 times larger than they do at present. The different forms of land use described above have often been used, separately or in combination, by groups or even individuals or families.

The Maya, for example, in their contemporary form and anciently, practice not only slash and burn but highly intensive land form constructions, which anciently included the canalization and construction of narrow raised fields over areas now reverted to swamps (AMARU IV 1980:57).

The Chinampa System of Permanent Agriculture—Mexico

For the past decade, the *chinampa* system of permanent agriculture from central Mexico has been touted as the most promising example of permanent agriculture practiced by indigenous inhabitants of the Americas (see Gomez-Pompa 1978; Maier 1979; Gliessman, Garcia and Amador 1981). Attempts to export this system to Mayan communities in southern and eastern Mexico have failed, however. As a result, serious questions arise about deriving models of resource management from indigenous systems and transferring them to other indigenous *or* colonist groups.

Nations and Komer describe the chinampa system as follows:

> To create a chinampa system, the farmer digs narrow irrigation/drainage canals on three or more sides of a cultivation plot, then adds the excavated soil to the plot to raise it above the water table. The farmer maintains crop productivity by periodically dredging mud from the canals and adding it to the cultivation plots as organic fertilizer. Aquatic vegetation from the canals serves as "green manure,"-and fish that colonize the canals provide additional, high quality protein (1983:235).

Under ideal conditions, the canals are said to allow cultivators to both irrigate during the dry season and drain the plots during the rainy season. The year-round production potential from such plots allows for the timely production of food and cash crops. In addition, farmers can also plant trees along the edges of the canals to hold soil in place. By carefully selecting tree species, farmers "can produce additional food, fiber and fuelwood and create wind barriers and habitat for wildlife such as insect-eating birds" (Nations and Komer 1983:235).

According to those researchers touting the chinampa system of permanent cultivation, Mexico's Instituto de Investigaciones sobre Recursos Bioticos (INIREB) in Veracruz and the Colegio Superior de Agricultura Tropical in Tobasco have conducted experiments with chinampa plots which indicate that they can produce constant and abundant harvests on lands previously used only for pasture or wet-crop cultivation. INIREB's chinampa field tests demonstrated sufficient yields of food and cash crops on plots of 2,000 meters square to meet the needs of a family of five.

Proponents claim that chinampa production does not require machinery, insecticides or artificial fertilizers. "The system is also compatible with cattle production, since crop residues and weeds can be used as fodder. In turn, the cattle provide meat and milk, and their waste are added to cultivation plots as organic fertilizer" (Wilken 1969:215, cited in Nations and Komer 1983:235).

In 1987, the Inter-American Foundation contracted Mac Chapin to evaluate several resource management projects in Mexico that were considered promising for replication in other areas. Some of the projects had been supported in whole or part by the foundation; others had been funded in whole or part by other organizations. Chapin personally visited four chinampa plots and met with researchers and technicians who had been involved with all of the experimental chinampa plots and the areas where chinampa-like systems of agriculture were said to have been adopted spontaneously. His report (Chapin 1987) indicates that the success stories of indigenous management systems often promoted as near perfect should be investigated thoroughly.

Despite numerous claims to the contrary, the chinampa system never existed outside of the Valley of Mexico. Chapin describes the traditional chinampas as follows:

Chinampa beds were, and still are today, built of alternating layers of aquatic weeds, bottom muck, and earth packed inside rectangular cane frames firmly rooted to the lake floor. The "artificial islands" thus formed varied in size, ranging from 30 to 100 meters in length and 3 to 8 meters in width. Ahuejote trees (a type of willow) were planted along the banks of the chinampas to provide shade, and their roots formed living fences that anchored the beds more securely to the lake bottom. The narrowness of the beds assured that the water in the surrounding canals filtered evenly through the plots at root level. Soil fertility was maintained through regular applications of swamp muck, aquatic plants and manure. Canals one-meter to three-meters wide separated the chinampas, forming a network of isolated islands reachable only by water.

In a very real sense, the chinampa form of agriculture has represented a self-contained and self-sustaining production system for centuries. Until the last several decades, it demanded no significant capital inputs, yet maintained an extraordinarily high level of productivity year after year. A wide variety of crops, ranging from staples such as corn and beans to vegetables and flowers for the market, were mixed with an array of fruit from small trees and bushes. Abundant aquatic life, such as fish, salamanders, frogs, turtles, and all manner of fowl, added protein to the agricultural diet.

The system is, however, labor-intensive. As in prehispanic times, the primary agricultural tool remains the digging stick; and until recently, no chemical fertilizers, insecticides or fungicides have been used. The farming plots, which ideally have considerable selection of crops in perpetual rotation throughout the year, need constant tending, and the interconnecting waterways must be kept clear of mud and weeds (1987:5-6).

Due to a series of internal crises in Mexico — increased production of export crops, decreased production of food crops, failed colonization programs and a general deterioration of life in rural areas — the scientists at INIREB, looking for agricultural alternatives, resurrected the chinampa model.

It promoted biological diversity, thrived without chemical inputs and maintained high year-round production. This was no abstract conceptual theory that required exhaustive testing, but a living, functional system that had proved it could work (Chapin 1987:9-10).

Chapin visited chinampa experimental stations in Tobasco and Veracruz 10 years after they were started. The most ambitious project to transplant chinampas took place among the Chontal Indians of Tabasco, who lived in a swampy area where they "fished, hunted and farmed over wide expanses of swamp and dryland areas" (1987:11) which few other people cared about. After discovering the remains of prehispanic raised agricultural beds in the area, experts were convinced that chinampas were ecologically suited to the region. Furthermore, it was assumed that the chinampa system of agricultural production would lure the Chontal back to their prehispanic "roots." The Chontal were never consulted about the advisability or desirability of introducing the chinampa system into their area (1987:13).

To speed up the construction of the system of chinampa beds, the government brought in huge dredges which dug up the swamp bottom and deposited it in "piles" measuring roughly 30 meters by 100 to 300 meters. The natural order of mud in the raised strips was inverted — the richest soil was on the bottom and clay, which hardened like brick when exposed to sun and air, was on top. The beds were neither fertile nor porous enough to pull water to the roots of the crops. The irregular gauging of the swamp bottom by the dredges made it impossible for the Chontal to use dragnets for fishing around the beds (Chapin 1987:13-14).

A number of other problems arose (Chapin 1987:14-16). Researchers insisted on organizing collective work teams — because prehispanic Indians in Mexico were supposed to have done it that way — to undertake the work on the plots. Such communal efforts were foreign to the Chontal. Technical assistance and capital subsidies were heavy at first, with the Chontal paid for their work on the scheme. Fertilizer and organic matter were trucked to the site. None of the crops grown were local to the area or previously eaten or marketed by the Chontal. Large quantities of insecticides and pesticides had to be used to control the insects and weeds that descended on the crops. Crops had to be replanted when the advisors found that the area had a different agricultural cycle from the Valley of Mexico.

The real problems, however, "started when the vegetables began to ripen" (Chapin 1987:15). Despite all the technical inputs and the ongoing research on production, no one had bothered to determine whether a market existed for what was produced. Furthermore, no one had arranged to transport or sell the produce. The first harvest, consequently, was a disaster.

The Chontal disliked the fact that the beds were not connected and that they were difficult to reach from the village. Officials quickly corrected this oversight and thus effectively cut off the essential "flow of water through the canals, reducing the accumulation of silt and weeds needed to fertilize the gardens" (Chapin 1987:16).

By the early 1980s the project had continued to slide into disorder. At that time, the advisors allowed individual families to take over the 65 raised beds. Intensive cultivation of vegetables and other cash crops was abandoned in favor of subsistence crops — corn, beans, bananas and some fruit trees. These crops provide the Chontal with some of their subsistence needs while allowing them to earn income as wage laborers. Gradually some of the farmers are beginning to produce some crops for market.

According to Chapin the problems associated with the transfer of chinampa technology to the Chontal were not exceptions. "Nowhere in the country has the transfer of chinampa technology from the Valley of Mexico to the humid lowlands been successful" (1987:19).

According to Chapin, there are a number of lessons to be learned from the failure of the transfer of chinampas. First, the planners' objectives had little to do with the interests and needs of the farmers. Second, outsiders designed and implemented the projects without significant participation from farmers. "The technicians were preoccupied with the narrow technical task of implanting an agroecological model. They overlooked the wider social, economic and political context in which the farmers lived" (1987:19-20). Finally, after the technicians abandoned preconceived programs, as with the Chontals, and began listening to the users, the projects had a chance of succeeding. As Chapin points out, the main problem with the transfer of such management systems may stem from the attempt to transplant them in toto rather than to extract the guiding principles and adapt them to existing systems in each new location.

Research Priorities

1. What pre-Colombian agricultural systems exist, in whole or in part, that are already adapted to specific environments? Could such systems be resurrected?

2. Why were many pre-Colombian systems of permanent agriculture abandoned? What lessons can be learned for the new systems of permanent agriculture being developed for rainforest areas?

3. How do traditional, permanent agricultural systems differ from imported models? What are the environmental, social and economic implications?

Natural and Modified Resource Units

Indigenous peoples throughout Latin America's tropical rain forests recognize and utilize a number of natural and modified resource units. They do not make a clear-cut distinction between fields and forest or between wild and domesticated. They are all part of integrated systems of land management that have been ignored by most Western attempts at resource production in tropical forests in favor of single products. Indigenous inhabitants harvest essential subsistence materials through a combination of hunting, gathering, fishing and agricultural activities. As Posey (1981, 1982a) has noted, Western scientists find it difficult to understand the use patterns of such areas, much less to measure production. It is even more difficult, perhaps, to determine the impact of use on the area.

Indigenous people visit different ecological areas to obtain specific necessities. They visit areas where fruits or nuts are in season, for example. By watching the environmental changes in one area, they can determine changes in other areas — demonstrating their understanding of the interrelated aspects of their environment. When a group needs a certain type of wood, or bamboo for arrows, they will visit specific sites in the forest. In some cases the entire group travels; at other times only a few individuals make the journey.

In addition to utilizing naturally occurring concentrations of specific known plants or animals, indigenous peoples often plant desired forest crops near their permanent or temporary camps or along frequented trails. By increasing the concentration of those species, food supplies are not left to chance and the indigenous groups do not have to worry about transporting bulky supplies of food when they travel or move camp.

The Kayapó Indians of central Brazil systematically gather a variety of forest plants and replant them near camps and major trails to produce artificial resource concentrations that may be denoted as "forest fields" (Posey 1982a). They use at least 54 species of plants from these forest fields, including several types of wild manioc, three varieties of wild yams, a type of bush bean and three or more wild varieties of cupa. Transplanting wild plants into human-made, higher-density forest fields imitates a transitional process of plant semi-domestication (Posey 1985) and a type of ecological strategy largely overlooked by Western science (Posey et al. 1984:103).

Posey (1985) writes that human-made forest fields allow the Kayapó to travel for months at a time without using regular garden produce. By upgrading the utilizable species in forests, the Kayapó can travel more frequently to more sites with greater ease. Today, however, as a result of catastrophic population declines resulting from contact with explorers and colonists, only remnants of a more extensive system remain. Even so, a single, contemporary Kayapó village, by conservative estimate, probably has 500 kilometers of trails that average 2.5 meters wide and are planted with yams, sweet potatoes, many other varieties of edible tuberous plants, medicinal plants and fruit trees (Posey 1985).

As primary forests were cut around Bora settlements in eastern Peru, pristine forests became more distant and the utilization of secondary growth more important. As a result, Bora upgraded the secondary forest that was nearer to their homes, leaving the more distant, primary forests relatively untouched. Today, Bora are reluctant to leave these upgraded secondary forested areas, yet they want certain items that are usually only found in primary forests. As a result, Bora have begun to plant desirable hardwoods and useful palms in swidden and fallow fields (Denevan et al. 1984:354).

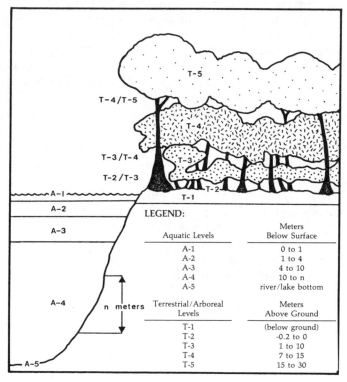

Fig. 8. Aquatic and terrestrial/arboreal vertical levels from an Amazon River *varzea* ecological zone near Coari, Brazil.
(Source: Parker et al. 1983:192)

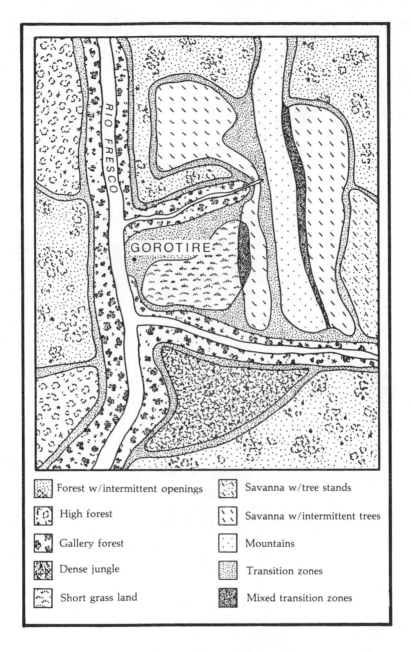

RIO FRESCO

GOROTIRE

	Forest w/intermittent openings		Savanna w/tree stands
	High forest		Savanna w/intermittent trees
	Gallery forest		Mountains
	Dense jungle		Transition zones
	Short grass land		Mixed transition zones

Fig. 9. Kayapó recognized ecological zones surrounding the village of Gorotire, Brazil.
(Source: Parker et al. 1983:172)

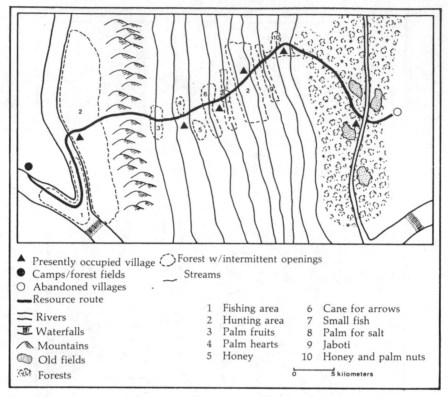

Fig. 10. Resource islands and campsites associated with "forest fields" utilized by the Kayapó of Brazil.
(Source: Parker et al. 1983:175)

Legend:

- ▲ Presently occupied village
- ● Camps/forest fields
- ○ Abandoned villages
- ▬ Resource route
- ≈ Rivers
- Waterfalls
- Mountains
- Old fields
- Forests
- ◌ Forest w/intermittent openings
- — Streams

1	Fishing area	6	Cane for arrows
2	Hunting area	7	Small fish
3	Palm fruits	8	Palm for salt
4	Palm hearts	9	Jaboti
5	Honey	10	Honey and palm nuts

0 ——— 5 kilometers

Indigenous groups are not the only ones that plant wild and domestic crops that upgrade the usable resources in a forest. Caboclos, too, recognize the importance of human manipulation in creating concentrations of important resources (Parker et al. 1983:183). Such caboclos have often spent years learning from nearby indigenous inhabitants how to sustain themselves in relatively fragile ecosystems. The success of caboclos in subsistence activities in tropical rain forests indicates that colonist populations, too, might be able to survive in such areas if they received sufficient instructions on location and were sensitized to local environmental conditions.

Scientists have only recently begun to realize that indigenous management systems in the tropics, taken in their totality — hunting, gathering, fishing and agriculture — are more complicated and better adapted to tropical conditions than previously assumed (Lovejoy and Schubert 1981; Posey 1983a:889).

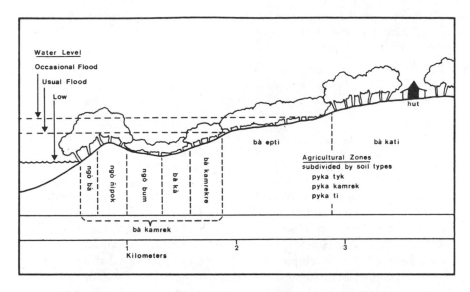

Fig. 11. Idealized cross-section of Kayapó-identified forest ecological zones and subzones near Gorotire, Brazil.
(Source: Posey 1983a:880)

> The tendency of Western science to analyze only those data that fit into neat categories tends to underestimate or miss entirely the importance of transitional categories of ecological explanation. This transitional system probably is much more widespread in Amazonia than expected and underlies the inadequacies of existing subsistence typologies and carrying capacity theories (Posey 1983a:887).

The upgrading of the forest for human use has probably occurred extensively throughout tropical rain forests, although little research has been done on it. Posey (1985) has found that of the presumably naturally occurring *apêtê* (forest patches/islands surrounded by savannas) most used by one Kayapó village in Brazil, at least 75 percent are made by humans. Creating apêtê requires hard work: sticks, limbs and leaves are piled into mounds until they rot and are then beaten with sticks into a mulch. The mulch is transported to slightly depressed, savanna sites where water collects and is then mixed with soil from termite mounds and ant nests. The new apêtê are about 0.5 meters deep and 1-2 meters wide. Over time they grow into considerably larger mounds, and are treated as gardens by the Kayapó. Posey estimates that the Kayapó can create apêtê of perhaps one hectare in 10 years. This practice could give great insight into aforestation and reforestation in tropical regions, but, unfortunately, little research has been undertaken on it (Posey 1985).

In many areas that were once the sites of permanent settlements, the human manipulation of species distribution is still evident and is, in fact, one way to determine sites of previous human occupation in tropical rain forests. Posey comments,

> but with data available, it is obvious that our ideas of "natural" campo/cerrado and forest must be re-evaluated with an eye toward the possibility of widespread aboriginal management and manipulation of these ecosystems. Perhaps the most exciting aspect of these new data is the implication for reforestation. The Indian example not only gives us new ideas about how to build forests "from scratch," but also how to successfully manage what has been considered to be infertile campo/cerrado (Posey 1985:144).

Under conditions of controlled population density, indigenous models of agroforestry systems do not deplete the natural resources of a region in the way that most imported models of development in tropical rain forests do. Evidence even exists that indigenous models of land use can actually stimulate overall growth and development of tropical rain forests when populations remain relatively stable and land rights are secure.

Indigenous methods of tropical resource management traditionally have required only low levels of technological inputs—they depend less on costly imported inputs than other agroforestry systems in the tropics. They do not need to generate many marketable items to reap higher net levels of income. When indigenous peoples come into more sustained contact with national/dominant societies, their number of material wants increases. As a result, such groups have often experimented informally with expanding traditional production strategies to include a larger number of marketable resources that are either grown, collected or hunted. Little research has been done, to date, on the transformation of traditional management and production systems of indigenous peoples. Research could provide alternative, better ways that their systems might be adapted to generate the levels of income that indigenous peoples or colonists now expect whether they live in formerly isolated areas or not.

Indigenous models of land use and management in tropical rain forests stress maximizing the number of crops produced in order to minimize the risk of crop failure resulting from conditions beyond the control of the producers. The rationale behind this form of land management resembles that practiced by peasants throughout Latin America; consequently, once the specific details of management in each area are learned, this alternative would be appealing to populations that might enter those areas.

Traditional economic theory indicates—based on notions of economies of scale—that larger quantities of one crop are more easily marketed than smaller quantities of many crops. All crops are not equal in value, however. Furthermore, such calculations ignore, or at least often underestimate, the economic costs of ecological destruction associated with monocropping systems of production in tropical rain forests.

Indigenous models of land use in the tropics depend on the rotational use of diverse plots of land — each with its own crop succession — which collectively provide the producer with a diversity of produce. Indigenous management systems that include tree crops, or even the selective planting of more preferred varieties, increase the length of time a plot can be used as well as the overall yields per land unit. The planting of choice wood species provides for the needs of future generations, as does the planting of various fruit or nut species, which extends the life of a plot for decades, even generations.

By maintaining the forest cover while increasing the proportion of fruit or nut trees, many indigenous groups increase the numbers of forest animals and fish, which in turn increases the availability of protein. The upgrading of natural forest cover through the planting of species which provide food or materials essential for other aspects of life, too, makes groups more self-sufficient by reducing the number of items either unobtainable or imported to the area.

A number of researchers have suggested that the manipulated and upgraded fallowing system of many indigenous peoples in Latin America is successful because it mimics the natural succession of forest reestablishment (Hart 1980; Uhl 1983:78-79; Denevan et al. 1984:354). Hart suggests that cultigens desired by indigenous cultivators are placed with their plots in niches that would normally be occupied by plants with similar growth characteristics and resource requirements. For indigenous plots, then, rice or maize are the analog crops, for

> early annual species, bananas replace wide-leafed Heliconia and late appearing tree crops mimic early successional tree species. Whether by accident or design, the Bora seem to follow this approach. Bananas do well in low shady areas, where Heliconia plants are also common. The most obvious example is uvilla which matches its ubiquitous cousin, the Cecropia. Guava is also in the same genus as its semi-domesticated analog, the shimbillo (Denevan et al. 1984:354).

Research should be undertaken to find desired cultigens that could substitute for naturally occurring species. Such research could identify potential food and cash crops for both indigenous peoples and colonists.

Some research among indigenous peoples indicates that the use and abandonment of forest plots may be crucial in the design of successful agroforestry systems. For example,

> Bora tree clustering according to local topographical conditions suggests that slope and terrain should be considered when planting agroforestry plots. More

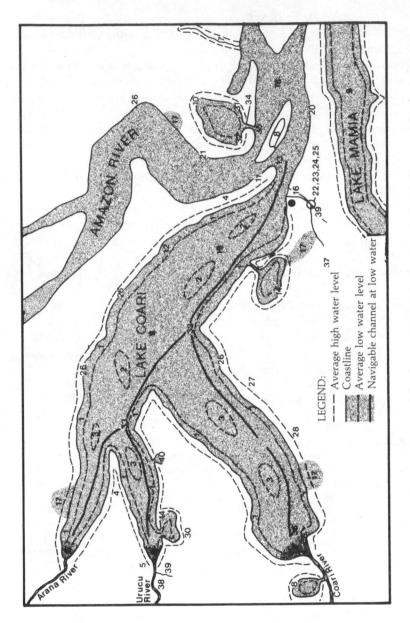

Fig. 12. Location of major resource units, and low-high water areas, in the Lake Coari area, Brazil. (Source: Parker et al. 1983:187)

Glossary of resource units appearing on Fig. 12, as defined by a caboclo of the Lake Coari region (numbers correspond to those presented on figure).

1. *praia branca* – dry season, white sandy beaches of Lake coari where birds and turtles lay their eggs.

2. *praia suja* – dry season, wet or muddy beaches where a great number of birds feed.

3. *praia verde* – dry season beaches, covered in short vegetation, where birds feed on weeds and insects.

4. *restinga* – natural river levees, usually covered in forest, and not inundated during the dry season.

5. *charco* – swamp area found within the várzea ecological zone.

6. *chavascal* – transition area between rivers draining into Lake Coari and the lake itself, characterized by low vegetation which is mostly inundated during the rainy season and which during the dry season forms a labyrinth of dead-end river-like branches, ressacas, pocos, and pocinhos surrounded by large areas of muddy land.

7. *igapó* – forest area which is flooded during the height of the rainy season.

8. *laguinho* – small lake connected to the river by a narrow stream during the rainy season, and only accessible by land during the dry season.

9. *lago grande* – large lake, such as Lake Coari or Lake Mamiá.

10. *lago* – lake connected to the river by a passage navigable by canoe or small boat.

11. *costa* – margin (bank) of the Amazon River.

12. *enseada* – gulf-like section of a large lake, usually characterized by calm waters.

13. *encontro das águas* – point where the Lake Coari water system flows into the Amazon River.

14. *poco grande* – deep section in a sharp turn of a smaller river, characteristic of the sinuosity of these rivers.

15. *ressaca* – lake-like formation connected to a small river.

16. *igarapé* – a black-water stream flowing from deep in the forest to a river.

17. *castanhal* – the terra firme forest where the catanheiras (*Bertholetia excelsia*) are located.

18. *águas fundas brancas* – deep white waters of the Amazon, where the piraibas (*Brachyplatystoma* spp) are caught.

19. *águas fundas pretas* – deep water areas of Lake Coari, associated with scarcity of resource except when in close proximity to the banks of the lake.

20. *barreiras* – high vertical banks of the Amazon River, characterized by swift currents and an abundance of clay varieties.

21. *embaubal* – section of the várzea where embaúba trees (*Cecropia* spp) are predominant.

22. *buritizal* – a concentration of buriti palms (*Mauritia flexuosa*).

23. *jauarizal* – a concentration of jauari trees (*Astrocarium jauari*) usually at critical zones during periods of medium water level.

24. *acaizal* – a concentration of acai trees (*Euterpe edulis*) in the terra firme.

25. *bacabal* – a concentration of bacaba trees (*Oenocarpus distinchus*) along igarapés.

26. *aratizal* – a concentration of arati bushes at the critical zone during periods of medium water level.

27. *capoeira alta* – an abandoned garden site more than ten years old.

28. *capoeira baixa* – an abandoned garden site approximately five years old.

29. *baixio* – shallow section of the Amazon River opposite the channel side, characterized by the predominance of oeirana trees (*Salix martiana*).

30. *tabocal* – a concentration of green-and-yellow bamboo (*Guadua* spp) in the high várzea.

31. *cananaral* – a floating meadow dominated by canarana (*Panicum spectabile*), commonly used as cattle fodder.

32. *muriruzal* – a floating meadow dominated by muriru (numerous species, see Smith 1981:14), providing food for both fish and turtles.

33. *canal seco* – navigable channel in the lake during low water.

34. *boca de cima (lago)* – point where a lake narrows into a stream before entering a river.

35. *boca de baixo (rio)* – point where the water from a lake flows into a river.

36. *matupazal* – a floating meadow dominated by matupá.

37. *rocado novo* – a recently planted slash-and-burn garden site.

38. *rocado velho* – a slash-and-burn garden site which is still being systematically utilized.

39. *igarapezinho* – a clear water rivulet which provides drinking water, also called a fonte.

40. *pocinho* – a small lake which does not dry up during periods of low water, usually located near ressacas and chavascals, and where fish are easy to catch by hand.

(Source: Parker et al. 1983:188-189).

important, slowly abandoning ground to secondary forest may be a sound strategy for tropical farming. There is no reason to think that agroforestry plots should have 100 percent planted standing bio-mass. Managed forest growth could provide useful products, as well as canopy cover for the soil and a source of stored nutrients for when the forest is cleared to begin the swidden and agroforestry cycle anew (Denevan et al. 1984:354).

Research Priorities

1. What overall effect does the manipulation or modification of rain forests (excluding agriculture) have on genetic diversity of rainforest flora and fauna? Does the manipulation of rain forests actually stimulate growth and diversity, as some experts suggest?

2. How many "pristine" rain forests have been, in fact, deliberately altered by indigenous people? To what effect? At what point does such manipulation affect genetic diversity?

3. What effect does a reduction of the land base have on the sustainability of such activities?

4. Among indigenous peoples living on the edge of rain forests and savannas, how common is the Kayapó system of creating rain forests? What do such practices teach us about the dynamics of rain forests or the costs of replacing them?

5. Which more valuable species could be substituted for species presently planted or otherwise encouraged by indigenous peoples and peasants who currently make a living in rainforest areas?

Indigenous Attempts to Establish Large-Scale, Sustainable Resource Management Systems

In the past two decades, indigenous peoples throughout the Americas have begun to organize at the village and at the national levels in order to take control of their lives and the destinies of future generations (see, for example, Macdonald 1985; Posey and Balee in press). These organizations have seen land rights and the development of sustainable systems of resource management as top priorities. In some cases, such programs involve the relatively straightforward but difficult task of obtaining legal title to the lands traditionally used. In other instances, programs involve working closely with outsiders to establish parks or reserves that overlap with indigenous areas, thus protecting the resource base of the group and the world as a whole. In some cases, indigenous groups hire outsiders as consultants to assist them in evaluating their options and proposing appropriate alternatives that not only meet the material needs of this generation but will continue to do so for future ones.

Some activities proposed by indigenous peoples as projects involve the modification of existing systems. For example, the Huichol Indians of Mexico had been selling logging concessions to timber companies (Leon 1984). They realized that if present cutting rates were allowed to continue they would soon deforest their land. With the assistance of a forestry specialist in a local university, they developed a plan to harvest their own trees and add value to the lumber by making items for sale. This program allowed the Huichol to selectively cut their timber, ridding the area of damaged or diseased trees, while increasing employment opportunities on their own land. By processing the wood themselves, the Huichol now earn 300 times more from each log that is harvested. This means that both their income and forests have increased dramatically. Furthermore, a 10 percent levy on all income from the sale of furniture goes toward communal projects (schools, health care) for the participating villages.

Three other indigenous initiatives are described below. However, hundreds of similar projects deserve description and analysis.

CRIC—Environmental Restoration in Cauca, Colombia

CRIC, the indigenous council in the Department of Cauca, is composed of 56 Indian community councils. The organization was formed in 1971 to protect Indian lands, culture and human rights. Cauca, with one of Colombia's highest concentrations of Indians, is located in the southwest part of the country. The original forest cover was destroyed long ago by mining and cattle ranching. Its eroded lands and impoverished population stand in contrast to the Cauca River valley — the site of the largest, most prosperous sugar plantations in Colombia.

As the sugar plantations in the valley have expanded, poor peasant farmers have moved further up the hillsides into upland frontier areas, lands belonging to indigenous peoples. As a result, intense competition now exists over land that was both scarce and of poor quality (Chernela 1987c:72). Conflicts over land have attracted both government troops and guerrillas. In the past 15 years more than 100 Indians have been reported killed in the area.

In 1984 CRIC ranked environmental restoration as its first priority. CRIC, with a staff of more than 30 non-Indian specialists, makes sure that the indigenous communities retain control of the development that takes place in their areas. CRIC began its forestry program by establishing three tree nurseries, run by local communities, to supply seedlings to communities that agree to plant a minimum of 1,000 trees — all native species. One community has carried out nine reforestation projects in only two years. As Chernela writes,

> such projects are carried out by community members utilizing simple technologies. Consulting experts conduct an initial training phase in each community and visit the projects at intervals thereafter. Community trainees learn to recognize native species and their qualities, such as growth rates, required growing conditions and economic and environmental uses. Former trainees often teach others to collect, prepare and plant seeds. In addition, CRIC has prepare a simple manual for communities or individuals wishing to practice forest restoration.
>
> The reforestation program is a model for community resource management. Many formerly unskilled community members, trained initially by outside specialists, have become specialists themselves. They improve their skills by attending seminars in Bogota, and later lend their expertise to other communities. Outside specialists train community members, who then hand down those skills to the community. This process is slow, but it creates a sustainable project, eliminates problematic and costly dependencies and empowers a community with valuable skills (1987c:72).

Environmental education programs are important components of CRIC's approach to identifying and presenting alternative forms of resource management. CRIC recognizes that reforestation and conservation measures that ensure sustained use of resources offer long-term economic advantages over short-sighted, immediate returns. Currently, their major objective is the reforestion of watershed areas. In addition, CRIC is working with communities to plant shade and fruit trees as well as stands for firewood — a commodity now in short supply in many communities.

CRIC is also interested in luring wild animals back into the area through even limited reforestation projects. Some researchers indicate that small mammals and birds can be attracted to forest patches with as little as four hectares (Bierregaard 1987). If reforestation is undertaken throughout a given rea in conjunction with other conservation schemes, some ecologists predict that local populations of some species of animals might even reach commercial levels (Janzen 1986:809).

Training and outreach are important parts of CRIC's resource management programs. Four years ago, Indians trained in resource management and reforestation were invited to a non-Indian community to assist in reforestation and farming; today, the community is outspoken in its support for the Indians' methods and results.

In such artificially created forests, Chernela (1987b) writes, prospects for sustainability are good, providing (1) the patches are large enough, (2) species diversity is high and (3) gains from conservation are greater than the immediate needs for forest products and their sale. The last point seems the most crucial and the most difficult to predict. Replanted forests can provide fuelwood and protect watersheds, but what is the correct value to be ascribed to these functions? Will Indians (or any other residents, for that matter) come to the same conclusions — that is, that the long-term benefits outweigh short-term needs?

CRIC hopes to meet some of the needs of local Indians through its reforestation and management programs. Reforestation can protect fragile watersheds, provide fuelwood, protect soils from erosion and provide fruits and shade and materials for fencing. The measure of success of the program, as Chernel suggests (1987b:10), "will be not only the number of forests planted, and the efficacy of the forest in bringing about desired ends, but the increased demands from *cabildos* [communities] to participate in the program."

In another, related environmental program, CRIC recently began an experimental farm in the indigenous community of Purace. Some 30 years before, a mine exploded in Purace, burning and polluting a large area. Some lands remained hard and unproductive at the time the farm was founded in 1985.

Students from a local agricultural institute showed farmers how to prepare organic compost for fertilizer and then assisted them in its preparation. All manner of organic material, including crop residue, was used to restore the devastated soils. In 1987, eight communities attended rotating work days on the land. Some walked for as long as four hours to undertake the work. They harvested 10 different crops on this previously unusable land and surpluses (even of corn and wheat) were sold in nearby towns.

The Awa Ethnic and Forest Reserve—Colombia and Ecuador

The Awa-Coaiquer Indians occupy a tropical rain forest that straddles the Colombia-Ecuador border. In the early 1980s, the World Bank was considering funding a road-building and colonization project in the area. In 1980, Cultural Survival supported a land demarcation feasibility study with the Awa. By 1983, regional representatives from 13 Ecuadorian government agencies established an inter-institutional development commission for the area. One of the commission's first acts was the demarcation of the Awa-Coaiquer Reserve.

Cultural Survival's project director, Theodore Macdonald, Jr., writes (1986:33),

> In September 1984 Cultural Survival agreed to provide support to:
> 1. aid the Awa-Coaiquer and the Ecuadorian Agrarian Reform Agency (IERA) in demarcating and titling traditional Awa land (approximately 80,000 ha);
> 2. obtain citizenship identification certificates for the adult population and thus permit their right to land ownership;

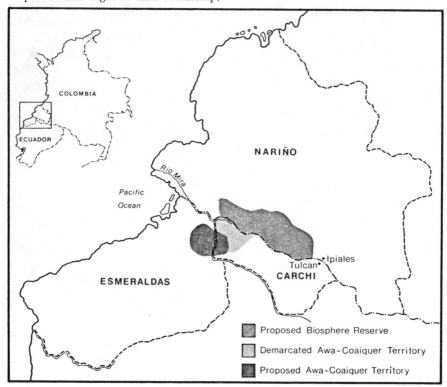

Fig. 13. Awa-Coaiquer Land Demarcation Project.

64   Indigenous Peoples and Tropical Forests

3. assist CONACNIE [National Coordinating Council of the Indian Nations of Ecuador] in establishing closer links with Awa communities;

4. provide logistical aid to CONACNIE and other support groups involved in training sessions aimed at informing the Awa of their rights within the national society and developing a pan-ethnic organization to exercise these rights; and

5. provide modest indemnification for agricultural production introduced onto Awa lands by colonists. The overall goal of the first phase of this project was simply to obtain legal title to the land Awa communities already use.

What results has the project produced? All 11 previously unorganized communities met and elected the Awa's first governing council. More than 1,100 citizenship cards were distributed; all but one small, isolated sector of Awa territory had been formally surveyed by March 1986. In the past three years, Awa Indian communities, the national Indian organization and several government agencies have peacefully collaborated and successfully obtained land for one of the nation's smallest and most isolated societies. With only limited assistance from the outside "the Awa have organized themselves into a political entity essential for the defense of their territory" (Macdonald 1986:34).

As Macdonald writes, this is, however, only the first step.

> Obtaining title and establishing a local political body to defend it is an important step toward cultural survival; guaranteeing permanent land tenure is another matter. Land that outsiders perceive as "idle" (i.e., not put to some obvious economic use) becomes a coveted parcel and an easy target once outsiders learn of its existence. In order to prevent confiscation of "idle" land, a management scheme or "development" project is essential.
>
> The Awa have already taken the first steps toward this end in order to protect their territory; a botanical research team from the University of Aarus (Denmark) undertook the first botanical survey of the area. . . . The research indicated that, similar to Colombia's Choco rainforest area, Awa territory is by and large ecologically undisturbed, and contains a wide variety of species whose distribution is limited to this particular area. Thus the area can be considered a "refuge zone" (i.e., one of several "islands" of tropical forest which remained as tropical forest during the driest period of the Pleistocene).
>
> Such refuge zones are considered extremely important research areas and, for that reason alone, it has been recommended internationally that they remain unmodified. Such arguments buy essential time for the local population to consider and develop a program of sustainable forest use and management, rather than simply concede to national development priorities that usually lead to extensive deforestation and cattle raising (1986:34).

In 1985 Ecuador and Colombia agreed to work together on an integrated program that would both preserve the fragile environment in the area and aid the Awa-Coaiquer. Each country has proposed programs that would combine Indian holdings into large reserves and a management program that would protect their habitat. In this instance, each country's expertise complemented the other's. As a result of intense contact with indigenous communities in the area, land rights in Ecuador were first guaranteed; only later did those involved begin to grapple with the problems of land-use programs. In Colombia just the opposite has happened. La Planada, a nature reserve, already existed as a major research site concerned with resource management, but it lacked the connections with indigenous communities that would allow its promoters to assess land-use patterns and needs.

The project has evolved into an example of international collaboration with regard to Indian rights and the controlled development of fragile ecosystems. The project demonstrates that Indian human rights, resource conservation and national economic development are compatible when combined in a program that is sensitive to the needs of the affected groups.

The Kuna Indians of Panama

The Kuna Indians of Panama recently established the world's first internationally recognized forest park created by an indigenous group (Chapin 1985; Chapin and Breslin 1984). This reserve, established with the assistance of the Inter-American Foundation, the Smithsonian Tropical Research Institute (STRI), CATIE, World Wildlife Fund-US and the US Agency for International Development, not only provides revenue to the Kuna from tourists who come to learn about the rain forest and from the sale of research rights to scientists, but protects and preserves an important part of the Kuna's heritage.

The Kuna Park has become a *cause celèbre* among environmentalists and indigenous peoples' rights advocates. There are numerous reasons for being cautious, however, about using the Kuna example as a model for other groups or areas. First, the 30,000 or so Kuna—living in more than 60 villages on small near-shore islands—never depended on internal forest areas to provide significant income or even space for subsistence agriculture. Vast stretches of forests have been left relatively untouched as the Kuna modified and managed shoreline forests and increasingly depended on the ocean, trade, and, more recently, employment in United States armed forces bases in the Canal area and near-shore agriculture for their subsistence and cash needs. Furthermore, the Kuna already prohibited agriculture, hunting and cutting trees in a number of spirit sites near their villages, although they did permit collection of items to be used for food and medicine. Thus, they experienced no fundamental conflict over restricting land use in rainforest areas, contrary to the experiences of many indigenous peoples.

Second, and also contrary to the experiences of most indigenous peoples, the Kuna already had title to the land in question. In the 1930s, through a series of armed uprisings, the Kuna forced the government to set aside this land for them. Since that time the Kuna maintained a strong political organization and united front in their dealings with outsiders. In this regard, the Kuna have controlled, from the outset, the design, implementation and management of the park.

Third, by the 1970s the Kuna became intensely interested in protecting their resources *and* their autonomy from outsiders who were encroaching on their lands. The new park — created as it was from relatively undisturbed rain forest and, better still, financed by a number of international organizations — served as an effective buffer zone between Kuna and outsiders.

Fourth, and finally, the Kuna are politically astute. They have a number of Western friends and advisors — some of whom they retain on contract — that advised them about the money-making potential of creating a rain forest reserve. With the help of these advisors, the Kuna obtained grants to help set up the resource base that would ensure income for decades to come. Yet through all the negotiations, the Kuna remained in charge. An indication of their adroit ability to manipulate the international concern for rain forests to their own advantage is their current desire to begin a campaign for endowment which will provide them with the resources necessary to develop a number of alternative income-generating schemes in tropical rain forests. Although the Kuna rain forests are far better protected than those of most indigenous people, they still might succeed in convincing a few international conservation agencies to support their work.

There is one area in which the Kuna have excelled from which other indigenous groups, or even countries, could learn: controlling access to research sites and demanding reports from researchers. The Kuna now require scientists to pay to undertake collections or research in their area. In addition, they require that all scientists leave reports of their activities *and* findings behind before they leave the area. Because STRI works closely with the Kuna and most scientists work in conjunction with STRI, they must comply. The Kuna ask that subsequent analysis and reports based on the information collected are sent to them as well. In addition, the Kuna require that each scientist take a paid Kuna assistant with them throughout their stay. In this way, the Kuna can keep an eye on the scientists, make sure they don't get hurt or lost, learn how different scientists collect information and observe inaccessible areas of the reserve in order to assess conditions there.

Research Priorities

1. One assumption many international assistance organizations make is that strong indigenous organizations serve as better protectors of a resource base than individual indigenous people. Is this assumption valid? Is it possible that new politically and economically oriented indigenous peoples'

organizations create parallel or splinter structures that undermine traditional, cultural organizations? Do these indigenous organizations lessen the responsibility individuals might feel toward their environment?

2. Indigenous organizations might be better equipped than individuals to secure and protect legal and land rights, but are they better equipped to discover new or modified productive components for existing resource management systems? To what extent do they control or structure the interaction between individual resource managers and outside organizations working to improve their management strategies and increase their income? Is this a problem?

3. To what extent does centralized planning and control of the economic activities of indigenous peoples living in biologic reserve areas permit individuals the freedom they need to undertake a broad range of resource management experiments? In a similar vein, which experiments — those conducted by individuals on their own lands or those designed and conducted by scientists — provide better information on which types of resource utilization strategies?

4. Biologists and agronomists exert control over most funds for research on alternative resource management strategies. How much can strong indigenous organizations become involved in positive ways in selecting appropriate research strategies and methods?

Conclusions

Indigenous land-use methods in the rain forests of Latin America resemble those of many traditional peasant societies: they stress a sophisticated and extensive knowledge of the local environment. They are based on the view that the environment is the source of life for future generations and should therefore not be pillaged for short-term gain and long-term loss. Agricultural technologies developed in mid-latitude farming areas — beginning with specialized agricultural machinery in the nineteenth century and expanding into seeds, fertilizers and pesticides in the twentieth century — have caused many of the world's farmers to view their land as their adversary, to be exploited and, if necessary, discarded. Those factors that allow for increased exploitation require, for the most part, cash investments, which in turn require intensified production. Farmers, then, are trapped in the middle of a vicious circle. It is doubtful that mid-latitude areas such as the Midwest of the United States can be used in this way for long periods of time; it is certain that Latin American tropical rain forests cannot be exploited in this way.

The resource management and utilization practices of many indigenous peoples throughout tropical rainforest areas can be combined with other strategies to develop more rational, long-term land-use patterns in the humid tropics. In the past, failure has characterized development projects in the tropical rain forest areas regardless of the size of the projects or technical inputs. New strategies with radically different approaches might allow for limited types of development in some rainforest areas. Although examining some specific indigenous systems of resource management provides useful information on local land use, these systems of knowledge fit within much larger cultural and social systems that may be impossible for most planners or colonists to accept. We do not yet know how much knowledge can be extracted from these management and land-use systems without destroying the way the entire system functions. Cultural prejudices aside, few colonists would be willing to live in tropical rain forests in a manner similar to traditional indigenous societies. By discovering the extent to which these traditional management practices can be altered, more cash crops can be generated to meet the increasing material demands of indigenous people as well as those of colonists.

The people that have used tropical forests for centuries without destroying them are now, in turn, being destroyed. A thorough understanding of their land-use systems and how these systems are being adapted in ecologically sound ways must be gathered before it is too late. Much of our understanding of indigenous models of land use and management are mere assertions that have been made — often by unqualified observers who, more often than not, have perhaps overly romanticized the qualities and capabilities of these systems. A few systematic studies have been undertaken by qualified research-ers and indigenous peoples themselves, however, which indicate that in-valuable understanding can be gained by pursuing these research topics.

The research that has already been undertaken gives us a clearer under-standing of indigenous systems of tropical rainforest management and use which can be sustained over generations. The following guidelines (Posey et al. 1984:891) for development in tropical rain forest areas can already be stated:

• Local agriculture must be adapted to the specific ecological zones and varia-tion of flora, fauna, soils and geomorphology.
• Agricultural development in rain forests should utilize more of the in-digenous cultigens that are already adapted to the environment.
• Fields should be small to prevent damage by insects, weeds and disease, dispersed to decrease their impact on the environment and planted with many crops which quickly produce a multilayered canopy that protects the soil.
• Various domesticated and semi-domesticated plants should be used to ex-tend the use of "abandoned" fields so that fewer areas will have to be cleared each year to provide the same quantities of food products.
• Research must begin to show the relevance of ecological balance to each individual living in a region so that all will have a stake in conservation.

Some of the most important areas for further research are:

• Indigenous knowledge of the interrelationship of flora, fauna, soils, topography and climate in specific ecological zones and between ecological zones.
• Specific systems of shifting cultivation adapted to each of these systems, examining the mix of native and introduced plants, subsistence and cash crops, and temporary and permanent crops.
• Evaluation of the ongoing experiments being undertaken by indigenous groups or individuals and their relevance to those being undertaken by scientists.
• Relationship between ground cover and the spatial distribution of crops within gardens for increased production and pest and weed control.
• Indigenous knowledge of the permissible density of cleared areas to forest regeneration, which maintains genetic diversity.
• Use of abandoned plots to increase the population density of wild plants and animals for hunting and gathering.
• Knowledge of indigenous populations about nutritional, medicinal and in-dustrial values of resources in their area.

In addition to these rather specific research tasks, four more general research topics should be included in the study of each specific indigenous land-use and resource management system:

• To what extent do indigenous models of land use provide for the present needs of the traditional inhabitants of Latin America's tropical rain forests without destroying the resource base?
• To what extent can indigenous models of land use be expanded to provide for the increasing material needs of the indigenous inhabitants of the rain forests?
• To what extent are indigenous models of land use acceptable to colonists to provide them with a sufficient level of income to meet their material needs?
• To what extent can indigenous models of resource management be transformed into current technology?
• To what extent will officials and planners be willing to accept lower production from rain forest areas in return for the maintenance of tropical rain forest ecosystems?
• To what extent do guaranteed land rights encourage the conservation of rain forests?

Further research strategies could be developed from this type of information. Scientists could use the specific case studies to classify different production systems according to the specific microenvironmental conditions and the perceived needs of the producers. General principles of indigenous management systems could be derived from these classifications and applied from one area to another through ongoing experimentation and evaluation. Once various indigenous systems of land use and their income-generating aspects have been identified, research can begin on those that are most productive, ecologically sound and of minimal risk to the producers. Information about upgrading traditional systems of management to meet current cash needs of both indigenous and colonist populations will make the adoption of new techniques and methods more acceptable to all people living in tropical rain forests. The survey of existing systems of agroforestry will allow planners to more realistically assess those carrying capacities that most effectively preserve tropical rain forests.

Examining indigenous methods of tropical forest use and management will hopefully inspire scientists to examine the productive capacities of those integrated systems that already exist rather than to experiment with individual inputs under ideal conditions. Most research conclusions, to date, are stated on a best-scenario basis; a worst-possible-scenario basis would perhaps reflect the more realistic concerns of the present or would-be occupants of Latin America's tropical rain forests.

Each indigenous culture that develops a sustainable relationship with the environment has a belief system that encompasses, among many other items, a set of rules about how the environment must be treated. Rituals and ceremonies in many indigenous cultures regulate the use of natural resources (Rappaport 1967, 1971; Reichel-Dolmatoff 1974, 1976, 1978). Reports have related food taboos with resource maintenance (McDonald 1977; Ross 1978a) and ritual cycles with seasonality (Reichel-Dolmatoff 1976). The relationship between social systems and resource management, however, is still not terribly clear.

An important issue not raised adequately by this review is the attitude of indigenous peoples toward their environment. Respect for resources is not universal among native cultures (a resource inventory of valued items is, in fact, a culturally specific list), but it is common. Respect for resources often reveals itself in such beliefs as the "sacredness" of the earth and the spiritual characteristics of aspects of the environment. Spiritual keepers of knowledge about resources, actual or potential crops or plants and game should not be dismissed lightly. Western attitudes, which stress the conquering of nature, have had disastrous consequences — at least when applied indiscriminately in tropical rain forests.

We do not yet know which resource management techniques can survive outside of their cultural settings and continue to function for settler or non-native groups in the area, or which can serve as models for production and management systems being established in environmentally distinct regions. Mac Chapin has observed that some groups, such as the Kuna of Panama, believe the rain forest is the "domain of potentially malevolent spirits which are prone to rise up in anger and attack entire communities if their homes are disturbed" (Chapin 1980:13). It is doubtful that colonists or planners could ever share such belief systems.

An examination of the systemic functioning of some of the indigenous methods of resource management in tropical rain forests might be a more efficient use of our time and energy at this stage. Some researchers have concluded that

> Scientists are competing with extinction in their race to inventory what the world contains. Amerindians are the only societies with the necessary knowledge, expertise and tradition to prosper in the Amazon jungle. Amerindians not only profoundly appreciate what exists, but also understand ecological interrelations of the various components of the Amazonian ecosystem better than do modern ecologists. Indians perceive specific relationships which biologists are only now discovering to be accurate. We remain in abject ignorance of the identity, location and mode of use of myriad Indian drug plants, cures for specific ailments, contraceptives, abortifacients, arrow poisons, and fish-stunning substances. Our ignorance of seasonality, migration and succession in the jungle is almost total (Goodland and Irwin 1975:65).

Although most Indian societies are already extinct, and those remaining face imminent destruction, there is still time to protect these people and to salvage knowledge about the Amazon from surviving indigenous systems. Research must proceed, however, with the utmost urgency and commitment, for with the disappearance of each indigenous group the world loses an accumulated wealth of millenia of human experience and adaptation (Posey 1983:891).

Such statements indicate, falsely, that the extinction of the indigenous inhabitants of tropical rain forests is inevitable. Indigenous people will most certainly continue to inhabit vast areas which are, at present, covered with rain forest. What is uncertain, however, is whether their rights to the land they occupy — guaranteed by virtually all the constitutions of Latin American countries — will be respected. If those researchers interested in developing sustainable systems of land use and management in Latin American tropical rain forests lobbied effectively for the land rights of indigenous people, they would help to maintain the largest population of people currently conducting ongoing experiments on land use in tropical rainforest areas. If, on the contrary, the same researchers insist on wringing information from indigenous peoples that will allow colonists, planners or government officials to usurp their traditional lands, then their research will certainly be thwarted by indigenous groups.

The extent of the conflict between indigenous peoples and colonists or researchers will depend on whether each group respects the rights and knowledge of the other. Within the context of this report, however, the economic self-sufficiency of individual communities and producers and their interdependence with the environment should be the underlying goal of all research and development projects in tropical rain forests. In this way sustained systems of management and production can be developed. These systems will not immediately generate the cash that many Latin American governments may hope for in the short term, but they will absorb moderate levels of population expansion and protect the largest, most fragile land environments in many of the countries in question.

References

Ackefors, H. and C. Rosen
  1979   Farming Aquatic Animals. *Ambio* 8:132-143.

Adams, R. E. W.
  1974   The Classic Maya Collapse: A Correction. *American Antiquity* 39(3):397.

  1982   Ancient Maya Canals: Grids and Lattices in the Maya Jungle. *Archeology* 35(6):28-35.

Adeyoju, S. K.
  1981   Agroforestry and Forest Laws, Policies and Customs. Paper presented at "Workshop on Agroforestry in the Humid Tropics," 27 April-1 May, Ibadan, Nigeria. Prepared by the United Nations University.

Agroforestry
  1981   Agroforestry in Venezuela. 2:3-4. Costa Rica.

Ahn, B. W.
  1978   Village Forestry in Korea. Paper presented at Eighth World Forestry Congress, 16-28 October, Jakarta, Indonesia.

Ahn, P. M.
  1959   The Principal Areas of Remaining Original Forest in Western Ghana and Their Potential Value for Agricultural Purposes. *Journal of the West African Science Association* 5(2):91-100.

  1979   The Optimum Length of Planned Fallows. In *Expert Consultation on Soils Research in Agroforestry*. pp. 15-39. Nairobi, Kenya: ICRAF.

Alcorn, J. B.
  1981   Huastec Noncrop Resource Management: Implications for Prehistoric Rain Forest Management. *Human Ecology* 9(4):395-417.

  1984   *Huastec Mayan Ethnobotany*. Austin: University of Texas Press.

Allan, W.
  1965   *The African Husbandman*. Edinburgh: Oliver and Boyd.

Allen, W. L. and J. H. Tizon
  1973   Land Use Patterns among the Campa of the Alto Pachitea, Peru. In D. W. Lathrop and J. Douglas, eds. *Variation in Anthropology: Essays in Honor of John C. McGregor*. pp. 137-153. Urbana: Illinois Archeological Survey.

Altieri, M. A. and J. Farrell
  1984   Traditional Farming Systems of South-Central Chile, with Special Emphasis on Agroforestry. *Agroforestry Systems* 2:3-18.

Altieri, M. A., D. K. Letourneau and J. R. Davis
  1983   Developing Sustainable Agroecosystems. *Bioscience* 33(1):45-49.

Alvim, P. de T.
  1972   Potential Agrícola da Amazônia. *Ciência e Cultura* 24:437-443.

  1978   Amazon Forest: A Balance Between Utilization and Conservation. *Ciência e Cultura* 30(1):9-16.

  1980   Agricultural Production Potential of the Amazon Region. In F. Barbira-Scazzocchio, ed. *Land, People and Planning in Contemporary Amazonia*. pp. 27-36. Cambridge: Cambridge University Press.

  1981   A Prospective Appraisal of Perennial Crops in the Amazon Basin. *Interciencia* 6(3):139-145.

AMARU IV
1980   The Once and Future Resource Managers: A Report on the Native Peoples of
        Latin America and their Roles in Modern Resource Management: Background
        and Strategy for Training. Washington, DC: AMARU IV Cooperative.

Ampuero, E. P.
1979   Ecological Aspects of Agroforestry in Mountain Zones: The Andean Region. In
        T. Chandler and D. Spurgeon, eds. Proceedings. Conference on International
        Cooperation in Agroforestry. pp. 77-94. Nairobi, Kenya: ICRAF.

Anderson, A. B. and D. A. Posey
1985   Manejo do campo e cerrado pelo os índios Kayapó. Boletín do Museu Paraense
        Emilio Goeldi. Belem, Brazil: MPEG.

1987   Reflorestamento Indígena. Ciência Hoje 6(31):44-51.

Andriesse, J. P.
1978   From Shifting Cultivation to Agroforestry or Permanent Agriculture? In
        Agroforestry. Proceedings of the 50th Symposium on Tropical Agriculture. pp.
        35-43. Bulletin.

Arellano, P. G.
1979   Ecological Aspects of Agroforestry in Arid Savannas: Venezuela. In T. Chandler
        and D. Spurgeon, eds. Proceedings. pp. 37-52. Nairobi, Kenya: ICRAF.

Arkcoll, D. B. and J. P. L. Aguiar
1984   Peach Palm (Bactro gasipaes H. B. K.): A New Source of Vegetable Oil from
        the Wet Tropics. Journal of Science, Food and Agriculture 35: 520-526.

Armillas, P.
1949   Notas sobre sistemas de cultivo en Mesoamérica: cultivos de riego y humedad
        en la Cuenca del Rio de las Balsas. Anales del Instituto Nacional de An-
        tropología e Historia 3:85-113. Mexico City.

1961   Land Use in Pre-Colombia America. In L. D. Stamp, ed. A History of Land Use
        in Arid Regions. Arid Zone Research. Volume 17. Paris: UNESCO.

Arnold, M.
1979   New Approaches to Tropical Forestry: A Habitat for More Than Just Trees.
        Ceres 12(5):29-37.

1982   Economic Constraints and Incentives in Agroforestry. Paper presented at UN
        Workshop on Agroforestry, 31 May-5 June, Freiburn, Federal Republic of Ger-
        many. Prepared by United Nations University.

Arnon, I.
1963   The Transition from Primitive to Intensive Agriculture in a Mediterranean En-
        vironment. World Crops 15(4):126-134.

Atmosoedaryo, S. and K. Wijayakusumah
1979   Ecological Aspects of Agroforestry in the Lowland Humid Tropics: Southeast
        Asia. In T. Chandler and D. Spurgeon, eds. Proceedings. pp. 117-128. Nairobi,
        Kenya: ICRAF.

Bailey, R. and N. Peacock
n.d.   Efe Pygmies of Northeast Zaire: Subsistence Strategies in the Ituri Forest. In I.
        de Gavine and G. Harrison, eds. Uncertainty in the Food Supply. Cambridge:
        Cambridge University Press.

Baker, D. C.
1982   Smallholder Farming in Sub-Saharan Africa. In C. K. Eicher and D. C. Baker,
        eds. Research on the Rural Economies of Sub-Saharan Africa: A Critical Ap-
        praisal. pp. 72-133.

Balee, W.
   1986a   Ethnobotanical Studies among Tupi-Guarani Speaking Indians in Amazonia. In
           *Discoveries in Economic Botany: Research and Results at the Institute of
           Economic Botany 1981-1986*. Bronx, NY: The New York Botanical Gardens.
   1986b   Ka'apor Ritual Hunting. *Human Ecology* 13(4):485-510.

Balee, W. and A. Gely
   1986   Utilization of Managed Forest Succession: The Ka'apor Case. In *Advances in
           Economic Botany* (in press).

de Barandiaran, D.
   1962   Activities vitales de subsistencia de los indios Yekuana o Makiritare. *An-
           tropologica* 11:1-29.

Barbira-Scazzocchio, F., ed.
   1980   *Land, People and Planning in Contemporary Amazonia*. Cambridge: Cambridge
           University Press.

Barney, G.
   1970   An Analysis of Swidden Agriculture in Southeast Asia. Ph.D. Dissertation, Ann
           Arbor, University Microfilms.

Barrau, J.
   1958   Subsistence Agriculture in Micronesia. *Bernice P. Bishop Museum Bulletin*.
           Honolulu, HI.

   1959   The "Bush Fallowing" System of Cultivation in the Continental Islands of
           Melanesia. In *Proceedings of the 9th Pacific Science Congress 1957, Bangkok*,
           7:53-55.

   1961   Subsistence Agriculture in Polynesia and Micronesia. *Bernice P. Bishop Museum
           Bulletin*. Honolulu, HI.

Barrett, O. W. and A. H. Verrill
   1937   *Foods America Gave the World*. Boston: L. C. Page and Company.

Basso, E. B.
   1973   *The Kalapalo Indians of Central Brazil*. New York: Holt, Rinehart and
           Winston.

Bayliss-Smith, T. P.
   1982a   The Ecology. In *Proceedings of the 9th Pacific Science Congress 1957, Bangkok*
           7:53-55.

   1982b   *The Ecology of Agricultural Systems*. New York: Cambridge University Press.

Bayliss-Smith, T. P. and R. G. Feachem, eds.
   1977   *Subsistence and Survival: Rural Ecology in the Pacific*. London: Academic
           Press.

Beckerman, S. and R. A. Kiltie
   1980   More on Amazon Cultural Ecology. *Current Anthropology* 21(4):540-546.

Beer, J. W. et al.
   1979a   A Case Study of Traditional Agroforestry Practices in a Wet Tropical Zone.
           Turrialba, Costa Rica: CATIE.

   1979b   Un estudio de caso sobre prácticas agroforestales tradicionales en el trópico
           húmédo: el proyecto La Suiza. Turrialba, Costa Rica: CATIE.

Bell, F. W. and E. R. Canterbury
   1976   *Aquaculture for Developing Countries*. Cambridge, MA: Ballinger Publishing
           Company.

Bene, J. G. et al.
   1976   The Tropical Forest: Overexploited and Underused. Research Priorities in
           Tropical Africa. Project Report to the President, IDRC. Ottawa: IDRC.

1977   Trees, Food and People: Land Management in the Tropics. Ottawa: IRDC.

Benge, M. and H. Curran
n.d.   Agro-Forestation in the Philippines. A US AID Information Paper. Washington, DC: US AID.

Beresford-Peirse, H.
1968   Forests, Food and People. Rome: FAO.

Bergeret, A.
1978   Ecologically Viable Systems of Production: Illustrations in the Field of Agriculture. *Wallaceana* 12:86-110.

Bergmann, R.
1974   Shipibo Subsistence in the Upper Amazon Rainforest. Unpublished Ph.D. thesis. University of Wisconsin, Madison.

Berlin, B.
1976   The Concept of Rank in Ethnobiological Classification: Some Evidence from Aguaruna Folk Botany. *American Ethnologist* 3(3):381-399.

Berlin, B. and E. A. Berlin
1977   Etnobiología, subsistencia, y nutrición en una sociedad de la selva tropical: los Aguaruna Jívaro. Mimeo.

Berlin, B., D. E. Breedlove and P. H. Raven
1973   *Principles of Tzeltal Plant Classification: An Introduction to the Botanical Ethnography of a Mayan-Speaking People of Highland Chiapas.* New York: Academic Press.

Berreman, G. D.
1979   *Himachal: Science, People and Progress.* IWGIA Document 36. Copenhagen: IWGIA.

Bhoja Shetty, K. A.
1977   Social Forestry in Tamil Nadu. *Indian Farming* 26(11):82.

Birley, M. H.
1982   Resource Management in Sukumaland, Tanzania. *Africa* 52(2):129.

Bishop, J. P.
1978   The Development of Sustained Yield Tropical Agro-Ecosystems in the Upper Amazon. *Agro-Ecosystems* 4:459-461.

1982   Agroforestry Systems for the Humid Tropics East of the Andes. In S. Hecht, ed. *Amazonia: Agriculture and Land Use Research.* pp. 403-416. Cali, Colombia: CIAT.

Bishop, J. et al.
1981   Dynamics of Shifting Cultivation Rural Poor, Cattle Complex in a Humid Tropical Forest Life Zone (Panama). Research note No. 2. Washington, DC: Development Alternatives, Inc.

Blandon, P.
1985   Agroforestry and Portfolio Theory. *Agroforestry Systems* 3(3):239-249.

Blank, P. W.
1976   Macusi Indian Subsistence, Northern Amazonia. Unpublished MA thesis, University of Wisconsin, Madison.

1981   Wet Season Vegetable Protein Use Among Riverine Tropical American Cultures — A Neglected Adaptation. *Social Science M.D.* 15(4D): 463-469. Austin: University of Texas.

Bodley, J. H.
1982   Resource Depletion and Territorial Requirement of the Shipibo of Peru. Mimeo.

Boom, B. M.
1985   Amazonian Indians and the Forest Environment. *Nature* 314:324.

1986   Ethnobotanical Studies of the Chacabo and Parane Indians. In *Discoveries in Economic Botany: Research and Results at the Institute of Economic Botany 1981-1986*. New York: The New York Botanical Gardens.

Boonkird, S.
1979   Agroforestry Practices in Thailand. In T. Chandler and D. Spurgeon, eds. *Proceedings*. Conference on International Cooperation in Agroforestry. pp. 145-148. Nairobi, Kenya: ICRAF.

Boonkird, S. et al.
1984   Forest Villages: An Agroforestry Approach to Rehabilitating Forest Land Degraded by Shifting Cultivation in Thailand. *Agroforestry Systems* 2:87-102.

Boserup, E.
1965   *The Conditions of Agricultural Growth: The Economics of Agrarian Change Under Population Pressure*. Chicago: Aldine.

Breedlove, D. E. ed.
1981   *Flora of Chiapas*. San Francisco: California Academy of Sciences.

Briston, M.
1965   Sibundoy Ethnobotany. Ph.D. dissertation, Harvard University.

Brokensha, D. W.
1982   Social and Community Forestry. *IDA* 1(2):3-7.

Brokensha, D. W. and B. Riley
1978   Forests, Foraging, Fences and Fuel in a Marginal Area of Kenya. US AID unpublished paper. Washington, DC: US AID.

Brokensha, D. W., D. M. Warren and O. Werner
1980   *Indigenous Knowledge Systems and Development*. Washington, DC: University Press of America.

Bromley, D. W.
1981   The Economics of Social Forestry. An Analysis of a Proposed Programme in Madhya Pradesh, India. Center for Resource Policy Studies, School of Natural Resources, University of Wisconsin, Madison.

Brookfield, H. C. and P. Brown
1959   Chimbu Land and Society. *Oceania* 30:1-75.

Brookfield, H. C.
1972   Intensification and Disintensification in Pacific Agriculture: A Theoretical Approach. *Pacific Viewpoint* 15:30-48.

Brown, C. H.
1972   Huastec Plant Taxonomy. *Katunob* 5(2):74-84.

Brown, C. H. et al.
1976   Some General Principles of Biological and Non-Biological Folk Classifications. *American Ethnologist* 3(1):73.

Brownrigg, L. A.
1981   Economic and Ecological Strategies of Lojano Migrants to El Oro. In N. Whitten, ed. *Cultural Transformations and Ethnicity in Modern Ecuador*. pp. 303-326. Urbana: University of Illinois Press.

Brunig, E. F., ed.
1978   *Proceedings of the IUFRO World Forestry Congress*. Djakarta, Indonesia.

Brunig, E. F. et al.
1979   Dependence of Productivity and Stability on Structure in Natural and Modified

Ecosystems in the Tropical Rainforest Zone: Preliminary Conclusion from the MAB-Pilot Project at San Carlos de Rio Negro for the Development of Optimal Agrosilvicultural and Silvicultural Systems. *Mitteilungen der Bundesforschungsantalt fur Forstund Holzwirtschaft* 124:41-50.

Brush, S. R.
  1973   Subsistence Strategies and Vertical Ecology in an Andean Community: Uchamarca, Peru. Ph.D. dissertation, University of Wisconsin, Madison.

  1975   The Concept of Carrying Capacity for Systems of Shifting Cultivation. *American Anthropologist* 77(4):799-811.

  1979   An Anthropological Appraisal of Latin American Farming Systems. *Studies in Third World Societies* 7:107-116.

Buck, L., ed.
  1980   *Proceedings of the Kenya National Seminar on Agroforestry.* 12-22 November, 1980, Nairobi. ICRAF and Nairobi University. Out of print.

  1981   *Proceedings of the Kenya National Seminar on Agroforestry.* 12-22 November, Nairobi. ICRAF and Nairobi University.

Budowski, G.
  1959   Algunas relaciones entre presente vegetación y antiguas actividades del hombre en el trópico americano. *Proceedings of the ICA* 33:213-229.

  1960   Tropical Savannas, a Sequence of Forest Felling and Repeated Burnings. *Boletín del Museo de Ciencias Naturales* 6/7 (1-4):63-87.

  1977   *Agro-forestry in the Humid Tropics, A Programme of Work.* Turrialba, Costa Rica: CATIE.

  1981   The Place of Agroforestry in Managing Tropical Forests. In F. Mergen, ed. *Tropical Forests: Utilization and Conservation.* pp. 181-194. New Haven, CT: Yale University School of Forestry.

Bunker, S. G.
  1980   Faces of Destruction in Amazonia. *Environment* 22(7):14.

  1981a   Class, Status and the Small Farmer: Rural Development Programs on the Advance of Capitalism in Uganda and Brazil. *Latin American Perspectives* 28[8(1)]:89-107.

  1981b   The Impact of Deforestation on Peasant Communities in the Medio Amazonas of Brazil. In V. H. Sutlive, N. Altshuler and M. D. Zamora, eds. *Where Have All the Flowers Gone? Deforestation in the Third World.* Studies in Third World Societies No. 13. pp. 45-60. Williamsburg, VA: College of William and Mary.

  1984   Modes of Extraction, Unequal Exchange, and the Progressive Underdevelopment of an Extreme Periphery: The Brazilian Amazon, 1600-1980. *American Journal of Sociology* 89(5)March:1017-64.

Burch, W. R.
  1982   Social Factors Affecting the Adoption of Social Forestry Techniques/ Technologies. Paper based on USAID Community Forestry Workshop, 12-14 July 1982.

Burgess, R. J.
  1981   *The Intercropping of Small Holders Coconuts in Western Samoa: An Analysis Using Multi-Stage Linear Programming.* Canberra: Australian National University Development Studies Centre.

Butt Colson, A. J.
  1977   Land Use and Social Organization of the Tropical Peoples of the Guianas. In J. P. Garlick and R. W. J. Keay, eds. *Human Ecology in the Tropics, Symposia of*

the Society for the Study of Human Biology. 2nd ed. XVI:1-17. New York: Halsted Press.

CAB
1975   Agriculture in Hill and Mountain Areas. CAB Annotated Bibliography No. 34.

Cabrera, L. G.
1943   Plantas curativas de México. Mexico: Ediciones Cicieron.

Campos, R.
1977   Producción de pesca y caza en una comunidad Shipibo en el Rio Pisqui. Amazonia Peruana 1(2):53–74.

Carlstein, T.
1975   Shifting Cultivation. Mimeo (cited in Townsend 1982).

Carneiro, R.L.
1960   Slash and Burn Agriculture: A Closer Look at Its Implications for Settlement Patterns. In A.F.C. Wallace, ed. Men and Cultures. pp. 229–234. Philadelphia: University of Pennsylvania Press.

1961   Slash-and-burn Cultivation Among the Kuikuru and Its Implications for Cultural Development in the Amazon Basin. In J. Wilbert, ed. The Evolution of Horticultural Systems in Native South America: Causes and Consequences, A Symposium. pp. 47-67. Caracas, Venezuela: Antropologica Supplement No. 2.

1978   The Knowledge and Use of Rain Forest Trees by the Kuikuru Indians of Central Brazil. In R.I. Ford, ed. The Nature and Status of Ethnobotany. University of Michigan Anthropology Papers No. 67:201-216. Ann Arbor: Museum of Anthropology.

1983   The Cultivation of Manioc Among the Kuikuru of the Upper Xingu. In R. Hames and W. Vickers, eds. Adaptive Responses of Native Amazonians. London: Academic Press.

Casanova, J.
1975   El sistema de cultivos Secoya. In Culture sur brulis et evolution de milieu forestier en Amazonie de Nord-Ouest. Basel, Switzerland: Societe Suisse d'Ethnologie.

Castetter, E. F. and W. H. Bell
1951   Yuman Indian Agriculture. Albuquerque: University of New Mexico Press.

CATIE (Centro Agronómico Tropical de Investigación y Enseñanza)
1979   Workshop — Agroforestry Systems in Latin America. Proceedings of Conference 26-30 March 1979. Turrialba, Costa Rica: CATIE.

Cavalcante, P.
1972   Frutas comestiveis da Amazônia. Vol. I. Belem, Brazil: Publicacões Avulsas do Museu Goeldi.

1974   Frutas comestiveis da Amazonia. Vol. II. Belem, Brazil: Publicações Avulsas do Museu Goeldi.

Cavalcante, P. and P. Frikel
1973   A farmocopia Tiriyo: estudio etno-botanico. Belem, Brazil: Museu Paraense Emilio Goeldi.

Centlivres, P., J. Gasdre and A. Lourteig
1975   Culture sur brulis et evolution deu Milieu forestier en Amazonie d'Nord-Ouest. Basel, Switzerland: Societe Suisse d'Ethnologie.

Central Arid Zone Research Institute (CAZRI)
1981   *Proceedings of the Summer Institute on Agroforestry in Arid and Semi-Arid Zones*. Jodhpur, India: CAZRI.

Cernea, M.
1981   Land Tenure Systems and Social Implications of Forestry Development Programs. World Bank Staff Working Paper 452. Washington, DC: World Bank.

Chagnon, N.
1968   *Yanomamo: The Fierce People*. New York: Holt, Rinehart and Winston.

1973   The Cultural Ecology of Shifting Cultivation Among the Yanomamo Indians. In D. R. Gross, ed. *Peoples and Cultures of Native South America*. pp. 126-142. Garden City, NY: Natural History Press.

1978   The Cultural Ecology of Shifting (Pioneering) Cultivation Among the Yanomamo Indians. *Proceedings of the 7th Annual Congress of Anthropology and Ethnology* 9:249-255.

1980   Highland New Guinea Models on South America Lowlands. In *Working Papers on South American Indians*. No. 2. pp. 113-130. Bennington, VT: Bennington College.

Chakroff, R. P.
1982   Preliminary Checklist of Socioeconomic Issues Related to Technical and Biological Components of Social Forestry Projects. Paper prepared after the USAID Community Forestry Workshop, 12-14 July 1982. Washington, DC: US AID.

Chambers, R., ed.
1979   *Institute of Development Studies Bulletin* 10(2).

Chandler, T.
1979   Documentation of Agroforestry Literature and Research. In T. Chandler and D. Spurgeon, eds. *Proceedings*. Conference on International Cooperation in Agroforestry. pp. 177-189. Nairobi, Kenya: ICRAF.

Chandler, T. and D. Spurgeon, eds.
1979   *International Cooperation in Agroforestry*. Bibliography. pp. 445-462. Nairobi, Kenya: ICRAF.

Change, J.
1977   Tropical Agriculture: Crop Diversity and Crop Yields. *Economic Geography* 53(3):241-254.

Chapin, M.
1980   Comments on the Social and Environmental Consequences of the El Llana-Carti Road, Republic of Panama. Washington, DC: US AID.

1985   UDIRBI: An Indigenous Project in Environmental Conservation. In T. Macdonald, Jr., ed. *Native Peoples and Economic Development: Six Case Studies from Latin America*. pp. 39-52. Cambridge, MA: Cultural Survival.

1987   The Seduction of Models: *Chinampa* Technology Transfer in Mexico. Unpublished report. November. Forthcoming in *Grassroots Development* 1988.

Chapin, M. and P. Brestin
1984   Conservation Kuna-Style. *Grassroots Development* 8(2):26-35.

Chapman, E. C.
1975   Shifting Agriculture in Tropical Forest Areas of South East Asia. pp. 120-135. IUCN publication #32.

Chaturvedi, M. D. and B. N. Uppal
1960   *A Study in Shifting Cultivation of Assam*. Delhi.

Chernela, J.
1982   Indigenous Forest and Fish Management in the Uaupes Basin of Brazil. *Cultural Survival Quarterly* 6(2):17-18.

1985   Indigenous Fishing in the Neotropics: The Tukanoan Uanano of the Blackwater Uaupes River Basin in Brazil and Colombia. *Interciência* 10(2):78-86.

1987a   Endangered Ideologies: Tukano Fishing Taboos. *Cultural Survival Quarterly* 11(2):50-52.

1987b   CRIC's [Consejo Regional Indígena del Cauca] Natural Resource Project. Unpublished project evaluation for Cultural Survival. August.

1987c   Environmental Restoration in SW Colombia. *Cultural Survival Quarterly* 11(4):71-73.

Chidumayo, E. N.
1987   A Shifting Cultivation Land Use System Under Population Pressure in Zambia. *Agroforestry Systems* 5(1):15-25.

CIPA (Centro de Investigación y Promoción Amazónica)
1979   *Etnicidad y Ecologia*. Lima, Peru: CIPA.

Clad, J.
1984   Conservation and Indigenous Peoples: A Study of Convergent Interests. *Cultural Survival Quarterly* 8(4):68-73.

Clarke, W. C.
1966   From Extensive to Intensive Shifting Cultivation: A Succession from New Guinea. *Ethnology* 5:347-359.

1971   *Place and People: An Ecology of a New Guinean Community*. Berkeley: University of California Press.

1976   Maintenance of Agriculture and Human Habitats Within the Tropical Forest Ecosystem. *Human Ecology* 4(3):247-259.

1977   The Structure of Permanence: The Relevance of Self-Subsistence Communities for World Ecosystem Management. In T. B. Bayliss-Smith and R. G. Feachem, eds., *Subsistence and Survival*. pp. 363-384. London: Academic Press.

Clay, J. W.
1982a   Deforestation: The Human Costs. *Cultural Survival Quarterly* 6(2):3-7.

1982b   A Typology of Social Forestry Projects — Where To from Here? Paper prepared after the USAID Community Forestry Workshop, Washington, DC, 12-14 July.

1985   Introduction — Parks and People. *Cultural Survival Quarterly* 9(1):2-5.

Clement, C. R.
1986   The Pejibaye Palm (*Bactris gasipaes* H. B. K.) as an Agroforestry Component. *Agroforestry Systems* 4(3):205-219.

Clement, C. R. and D. B. Arkcoll
1979   A politica florestal e o futuro promissor da fruti cultura na Amazonia. *Acta Amazônica* 9(4):173-177.

Cochrane, T. T. and P. A. Sanchez
1982   Land Resources, Soils and Their Management in the Amazon Region: A State of Knowledge Report. In S. B. Hecht, ed. *Amazonia: Agriculture and Land Use Research*. pp. 137-209. Cali, Colombia: CIAT.

Combe, J.
1979   Conceptos sobre la investigación de técnicas agroforestales en el CATIE. In Taller, ed. *Sistemas Agro-Forestales en América Latina*. pp. 49-57. Turrialba, Costa Rica: CATIE.

Combe, J. and G. Budowski
  1979   Classification of Agro-Forestry Techniques. In G. De las Salas, ed., *Proceedings.*
          Workshop on Agroforestry Systems in Latin America. pp. 17-47. Turrialba,
          Costa Rica: CATIE.

Conklin, H. C.
  1957   Hanunoo Agriculture. A Report on an Integral System of Shifting Cultivation in
          the Philippines. FAO Forestry Development Paper No. 12. Rome: FAO.

  1959   Shifting Cultivation and Succession to Grassland Climax. In *Proceedings of the*
          9th Pacific Science Congress, 1957, Bangkok 7:60-62.

  1963   *The Study of Shifting Cultivation.* Pan American Union Studies and
          Monographs VI. Washington, DC: Union Panamericana.

  1969   An Ethnoecological Approach to Shifting Agriculture. In A. P. Vayda, ed. *En-*
          vironment and Cultural Behavior. pp. 221-231. Austin: University of Texas
          Press.

  1980   *Ethnographic Atlas of Ifugao: A Study of Environment, Culture and Society in*
          Northern Luzon. New Haven, CT: Yale University Press.

Contant, R. B.
  1980   Training and Education in Agroforestry. In T. Chandler and D. Spurgeon, eds.
          International Cooperation in Agroforestry. Nairobi, Kenya: ICRAF/DSE.

Contreras, R. C.
  1936   *50 plantas medicinales indígenas.* 2nd ed. Mexico.

Conzemius, E.
  1932   *Ethnographical Survey of the Miskito and Sumu Indians of Honduras and*
          Nicaragua. BAE Bulletin No. 106. Washington, DC: Smithsonian Institute.

Cook, O. F.
  1921   Milpa Agriculture: A Primitive Tropical System. In *Annual Report of the*
          Smithsonian Institution for 1919. Washington, DC: US Government Printing
          Office.

Cooley, J. H. and F. B. Golley
  1984   *Trends in Ecological Research for the 1980s.* New York: Plenum Press.

Corley, R. H. V.
  1983   Potential Productivity of Tropical Perennial Crops. *Explorations in Agriculture*
          19:217-237.

Cosminsky, S.
  1978   Medicinal Plants of the Black Caribs. In *Proceedings of the 42nd ICA, 1976.*

Covich, A. P. and N. H. Nickerson
  1966   Studies of Cultivated Plants in Choco Dwelling Clearings, Darien, Panama.
          Economic Botany 20:285-301.

Crosse-Upcott, A. R. W.
  1958   Ngindo Famine Subsistence. *Tanganyika Notes and Records* 50:120.

Cuevas, B.
  1913   *Plantas medicinales de Yucatán.* Merida, Mexico.

Cultural Survival
  1980   Cultural Survival Projects—A Review: Brazil-Suruí Economic Development.
          Cultural Survival Newsletter 5(4):20.

  1982   Deforestation: The Human Costs. *Cultural Survival Quarterly* 6(2).

Daccarett, M. and J. Blydenstein
  1968   *The Influence of Leguminous and Nonleguminous Trees on the Forage That*
          Grows Beneath Them. Turrialba, Costa Rica: CATIE. 18(4):405-408.

Dagon, R. R.
  1967   Current Agricultural Practices Among the WaiWai. Montreal: McGill University
          Savanna Research Series 8.

Denevan, W. M.
  1966   A Cultural Ecological View of the Former Aboriginal Settlement in the Amazon
          Basin. *The Professional Geographer* 15(6):346-351.

  1970   Aboriginal Drained-Field Cultivation in the Americas. *Science* 169:647-654.

  1971   Campa Subsistence in the Gran Pajonal, Eastern Peru. *The Geographical Review*
          61(4):496-518.

  1973   Development and the Imminent Demise of the Amazon Rain Forest. *The Profes-
          sional Geographer* XXV:130-135.

  1978   The Causes and Consequences of Shifting Cultivation in Relation to Tropical
          Forest Survival. Paper presented at the Congreso Internacional de Geografos
          Latinoamericanistas, 3-9 August 1977, Paipa, Colombia. In *Proceedings* 7:67-81.

  1980   Swiddens and Cattle Versus Forest: The Imminent Demise of the Amazon Rain
          Forest Reexamined. *Studies in Third World Societies* 13:25-44.

Denevan, W. M. and R. W. Bergman
  1975   Karinya Indian Swamp Cultivation in the Venezuelan Llanos. *Yearbook of the
          Association of Pacific Coast Geographers* 37:23-37.

Denevan, W. M. and K. H. Schwerin
  1980   Adaptive Strategies in Karinya Subsistence, Venezuelan Llanos. *Antropologica*
          50:3-91.

Denevan, W. M., J. M. Treacy and J. B. Alcorn
  1984   Indigenous Agroforestry in the Peruvian Amazon: The Example of Bora Utiliza-
          tion of Swidden Fallows. In J. Hemming, ed. *Change in the Amazon Basin.*
          Manchester, England: University of Manchester.

Denevan, W. M. et al.
  1984a   Indigenous Agroforestry in the Northwest Peruvian Amazon. Project report,
          Consortium for the Study of Man's Relationship to his Global Environment.

  1984b   Indigenous Agroforestry in the Peruvian Amazon: Bora Indian Management of
          Swidden Fallows. *Interciencia* 9(6):346-357.

DEVRES
  1980   *The Socio-Economic Context of Fuelwood Use in Small Rural Communities.*
          USAID. Evaluation Special Studies No. 1. Washington, DC: USAID.

DeWalt, B.
  1982   The Big Macro Connection: Population, Grain and Cattle in Southern Hon-
          duras. *Culture and Agriculture* 14/Winter:1-12.

Dickinson III, J. C.
  1972   Alternatives of Monoculture in the Humid Tropics of Latin America. *The Pro-
          fessional Geographer* 24(3):217-222.

Donkin, R. A.
  1979   *Agricultural Terracing in the Aboriginal New World.* Tucson: University of
          Arizona Press.

Dougall, H. W. and A. V. Bogdan
  1957   Browse Plants of Kenya with Special Reference to Those Occuring in South Bar-
          ingo. *The East African Agricultural Journal.* pp. 236-245.

Douglas, J. S. and R. A. de J. Hart
  1976   *Forest Farming: Towards a Solution to Problems of World Hunger and Conser-
          vation.* London: Watkins.

Dove, M. R.
1983   Theories of Swidden Agriculture and the Political Economy of Ignorance. *Agroforestry Systems* 1(2):85-100.

Dubois, J.
1979   Aspects of agroforestry systems in Mayombe and Lower Congo (Zaire). In *Workshop: Agroforestry Systems in Latin America.* pp. 84-90. Turrialba, Costa Rica: CATIE.

Duke, J.
1975   Ethnobotanical Observations of the Cuna Indians. *Economic Botany* 29:278-293.

Dumond, D. E.
1969   Swidden Agriculture and the Rise of Maya Civilization. In A. P. Vayda, ed. *Environment and Cultural Behavior.* pp. 332-349. Austin: The University of Texas.

Eckholm, E. P. et al.
1975   Growing Food in the Tropical Forests: No Bread Basket in the Jungle. *Development Forum* 3(6):6-7.

Eckholm, E. and L. R. Brown
1977   *Spreading Deserts: The Hand of Man.* World Watch Paper No. 13. Washington DC: World Watch Institute.

Eden, M. J.
1974   Ecological Aspects of Development Among Piaroa and Guahibo Indians of the Upper Orinoco Basin. *Antropologica* 39:25-56.

1978   Ecology and Land Development: The Case of Amazonian Rainforests. In *Transactions of the Institute of British Geographers.* New Series 3(7):444-463.

1980   A Traditional Agro-System in the Amazon Region of Colombia. In J. I. Furtado, ed. *Tropical Ecology and Development.* Proceedings, Fifth International Symposium in Tropical Ecology. 1:509-514.

Edens, T. C. and H. E. Koenig
1980   Agro-ecosystems Management in a Resource Limited World. *BioScience* 30:697-701.

Eder, J.
1977   Agricultural Intensification and the Returns to Labour in the Philippine Swidden System. *Pacific Viewpoint* 19:1-21.

Egger, K.
1978   Eco-farming: Entwicklungstrategi fur problemgebiete? *Entwicklung Landlicher Raum* 12(2):10-14.

1978   Eco-farming — Kern oekologisher Agrarentwicklung? *Entwicklung and Zusammenarbeit* 8/9:22-24.

Eilers, H.
1985   Protected Areas and Indigenous Peoples. *Cultural Survival Quarterly* 9(1):6-9.

Elisabetsky, E. and D. Posey
1987a   Pesquisa etnofarmacologica e recursos naturais no tropico umido: O caso dos índios Kayapó e suas implicacões para a ciência medica. First symposium on the Humid Tropics. Belem, Brazil: EMBRAPA/CPATU.

1987b   Etnofarmacologia dos índios Kayapó do Gorotire. *Revista Brasileira Zoologica.*

Escalante, E.
1985   Promising Agroforestry Systems in Venezuela. *Agroforestry Systems* 3(2):209.

Escalante, E., S. Benacchio and H. Reyes
1979   Research on Production Systems in the Barlovento Region, Cuagua, Venezuela. Workshop. pp. 101-106.

Etherington, D. M. and M. J. Matthews
   1983   Approaches to the Economic Evaluation of Agroforestry Farming Systems. *Agroforestry Systems* 1:347-360.

Ewel, J. et al.
   1981   Leaf Area, Light Transmission, Roots and Leaf Damage in Tropical Plant Communities. *Agro-Ecosystems*. (4):305-326.

Ewell, P. T. and T. Poleman
   1980   *Uxpanapa: Agricultural Development in the Mexican Tropics*. New York: Pergamon Press.

Ewell, P. T. et al.
   n.d.   Tropical Agro-Ecosystem Structure. *Agro-Ecosystems*. in press.

FAO (Food and Agriculture Organization)
   1957   Shifting Cultivation. An appeal by FAO to governments, research centers, associations and private persons who are in a position to help. *Unasylva* 11.

   1969   Shifting Cultivation in Tropical Forest: Summary. Rome: FAO. 14 pages.

   1977   Forestry in Uttar Pradesh: The Hugging the Trees Movement. *Ideas and Action Bulletin* 116:20-21.

   1978a   Shifting Cultivation. *Forest News for Asia and the Pacific* 1(2):1-16.

   1978b   Forest Influences: An Introduction to Ecological Forestry. Rome: FAO (original 1962).

FAO/CHDF(Corporacion Hondureno de Desarrollo Forestal)
   1980   *El uso de incentivos para actividades forestales y de conservación en comunidades en Honduras*. Tegucigalpa: CHDF.

FAO/SIDA (Swedish International Development Authority)
   1974   Shifting Cultivation and Soil Conservation in Africa. *FAO Soils Bulletin* No. 24.

Fearnside, P. M.
   1979   The Development of the Amazon Rainforest: Priority Problems for the Formulation of Guidelines. *Interciência* 4(6):338-342.

Federov, A. A.
   1966   The Structure of the Tropical Rain Forest and Speciation in the Humid Tropics. *Journal of Ecology* 54:1-11.

Felger, R. S.
   1977   Mesquite in Indian cultures of southern North America. In B. B. Simpson, ed. *Mesquite: Its Biology in Two Desert Scrub Ecosystems*. Stroudsburg, PA: Hutchinson and Ross.

Felger, R. S. and G. P. Nabban
   1978   Agroecosystem Diversity: A Model from the Sonoran Desert. In N. L. Gonzales, ed. *Social and Technological Management in Dry Lands*. Boulder, CO: Westview Press.

Fernandes, E. C. M. and P. K. R. Nair
   1986   An Evaluation of the Structure and Function of Some Tropical Homegardens. *Agricultural Systems* 21:179-310.

Filius, A. M.
   1981   Economic Aspects of Agroforestry. In K. F. Wiersum, ed. *Viewpoints on Agroforestry*. The Netherlands: Agricultural University at Wageningen.

Fittkau, E. J.
   1973   Crocodiles and the Nutrient Metabolism of Amazonian Waters. *Amazonia* 5(1):103-133.

Fittkau, E. J. et al., eds.
1968   Biogeography and Ecology in South America. *Den Haag, Mongraphiae Biologicae* 18/19.

Flannery, K. V., ed.
1982   *Maya Subsistence*. New York: Academic Press.

Fliervoet, E.
n.d.   An Inventory of Trees and Shrubs in the Northern Division of Machakos District, Kenya. The Netherlands: ICRAF/Wageningen Agricultural University.

Forde, C. D.
1934   The Bora of the Western Amazon Forest. In C. D. Forde. *Habitat, Economy and Society*. pp. 131-147. London: Methuen.

Fox, R. G.
1969   Professional Primitives: Hunters and Gatherers of Nuclear South Asia. *Man in India* 49(2):139-160.

Frechione, J.
1981   Economic Self-Development by Yekuana Amerinds in Southern Venezuela. Ph.D. Dissertation, University of Pittsburgh, Pennsylvania.

1984   The Yekuana of Southern Venezuela. *Cultural Survival Quarterly* 8(4):22-25.

Frikel, P.
1959   Agricultura dos Indios Munduruku. *Boletím do Museu Paraense Emilio Goeldi* 4. Belem, Brazil.

1971   A tecnica da roca dos índios mundurucú. In C. Rocque, ed. *Antologia da Cultura Amazônica* 6:132-136. Sao Paulo.

Fuchs, H.
1962   *El sistema de cultivo de los Makiritare (Deukwhuana) del Alto Ventuari, Territorio Federal Amazonas, Venezuela*. Proceedings of the 35th Congress of the ICA.

Furtado, J. I., ed.
1980   *Tropical Ecology and Development*. Kuala Lumpur: International Society for Tropical Ecology.

Galvao, E.
1963   Elementos básicos da horticultura de subsistencia indígena. *Revista do Museu Paulista* 14:120-144.

Galvao, A. P. M.
1979   Ecological Aspects of Agroforestry in the Humid Tropics: The Brazilian Amazon. In T. Chandler and D. Spurgeon, eds. *Proceedings*. Conference on International cooperation in Agroforestry. pp. 109-116. Nairobi, Kenya: ICRAF.

Gasche, J.
1979   Cultivo de corte y quema y evolución del medio forestal en el noroeste del Amazonas: ecología de los sistemas de cultivo indígenas en la selva peruana. Paris: Centre National de la Recherche Scientifique. Mimeo.

1980   El estudio comparativo de los sistemas de cultivo nativos y su impacto sobre el bosque amazónico. In *Consulta científica subregional sobre las actividades de Corte y Quema en el ecosistema de Bosque Tropical*. pp. 61-74. Iquitos, Peru: MAB.

Geertz, C.
1963   *Agricultural Involution: The Process of Ecological Change in Indonesia*. Berkeley: University of California Press.

1969   Two Types of Ecosystems. In A. P. Vayda, ed. *Environment and Cultural Behavior*. pp. 3-28. Austin: University of Texas Press.

Getahun, A.

1977   Raising the Productivity of Peasant Agriculture in Ethiopia. *AAASA Journal* IV(1):27-40.

1979   Ecological Aspects to Agroforestry in the Highland Ecosystems of Tropical Africa. In T. Chandler and D. Spurgeon, eds. *Proceedings.* Conference on International Cooperation in Agroforestry. pp. 95-107. Nairobi, Kenya: ICRAF.

1981   *Preliminary Inventory of Useful Plants of the Humid Zones of Nigeria.* Ibadan, Nigeria: IITA.

Gielen, H.

n.d.   *Report on agroforestry survey in three villages of Northern Machakos, Kenya.* The Netherlands: ICRAF Wagnineen Agricultural University.

Gill, T.

1967   *Shifting Agriculture: New Aspects of an Old Problem.* pp. 10-22. Rome: FAO.

Gliessman, S. R. and A. M. Amador

1980   Ecological Aspects of Production in Traditional Agroecosystems in the Humid Lowland Tropics of Mexico. In J. I. Furtado, ed. *Tropical Ecology and Development.* pp. 601-608. Kuala Lumpur: International Society for Tropical Ecology.

1982   Review of Ewell 1980. *Economic Geography* 58(1):93-94.

Glover, N. and J. Beer

1986   Nutrient Cycling in Two Traditional Central American Agroforestry Systems. *Agroforestry Systems* 4(2):77-88.

Goldman, I.

1963   *The Cubeo, Indians of the Northwest Amazon.* Urbana: University of Illinois Press.

1981   Cubeo Dietary Rules. Working Papers on South America No. 3. pp. 144-156. Bennington, VT: Bennington College.

Golley, F. B.

1983   *Tropical Rain Forest Ecosystems: Structure and Function.* New York: Elsevier Scientific Publishing Company.

Golley, F. B. and E. B. Farnworth, eds.

1974   *Fragile Ecosystems: Evaluation of Research and Applications in the Neotropics.* New York: Springer-Verlag.

Golley, F. B. and E. Medina

1975   *Tropical Ecological Systems: Trends in Terrestrial and Aquatic Research.* New York: Springer-Verlag.

Gomez-Pompa, A.

1978   Vino nuevo en odre viejo. *Mazingira* 5:49-55.

Gomez-Pompa, A., C. Vazquez-Yanes and S. Guevam

1972   The Tropical Rainforest: A Non-Renewable Resource. *Science* 177:762-765.

Gomez-Pompa, A. et al.

1982   Experiences in Traditional Hydraulic Agriculture. In K. V. Flannery, ed. *Maya Subsistence.* pp. 327-342. New York: Academic Press.

Goodland, R.

1980   Environmental Ranking of Amazonian Development Projects in Brazil. *Environmental Conservation* 7(1):9-26.

Goodland, R. and J. Bookman

1977   Can Amazonia Survive Its Highways? *Ecologist* 7:376-380.

Goodland, R., H. S. Irwin and G. Tillman

1978   Ecological Development for Amazonia. *Ciência e Cultura* 30(3):275-289.

Gordon, B. L.
    1969   Anthropogeography and Rainforest Ecology in Bocas del Tora Province, Panama. Office of Naval Research Report. Berkeley: University of California.

    1982   *A Panama Forest and Shore: Natural History and Amerindian Culture in Bocas del Toro.* Pacific Grove, CA: Boxwood Press.

Gottlieb, O. R.
    1981   New and Under-Utilized Plants in the Americas: Solution to Problems of Inventory Through Systematics. *Interciência* 6(1):22-29.

Goulding, M.
    1980   *Fishes and the Forest: Explorations in Amazonian Natural History.* Berkeley: University of California Press.

    1983   Amazonian Fisheries. In E. Moran, ed. *The Dilemma of Amazonian Development.* pp. 189-210. Boulder, CO: Westview Press.

Grainger, A.
    1980   The Development of Tree Crops and Agroforestry Systems. *International Tree Crops Journal* 1:3-34.

Grandstaff, T. B.
    1977   The Development of Traditional Swidden (Shifting Cultivation) Systems in the Marginal Mountain Areas of North Thailand: A Case Study.

    1980   Shifting Cultivation in Northern Thailand: Possibilities for Development. Resources Systems Theory and Methodology Series No. 3. Tokyo: United Nations University.

    1983   *Shifting Cultivation in Northern Thailand: Possibilities for Development.* Tokyo: United Nations University.

Gray, S. G.
    1970   The Place of Trees and Shrubs as Sources of Forage in Tropical and Subtropical Pastures. *Tropical Grasslands* 4:57-62.

Greenberg, A. M.
    1985   Game Conservation and Native Peoples in Northern Ontario. *Cultural Survival Quarterly* 9(1):26-30.

Greenland, D. J.
    1975   Bringing the Green Revolution to the Shifting Cultivator: Better Seed, Fertilizers, Zero or Minimum Tillage and Mixed Cropping Are Necessary. *Science* 190(4217):841-844.

Gross, D.
    1975   Protein Capture and Cultural Development in the Amazon Basin. *American Anthropologist* 77(3):526-549.

Gross, D. et al.
    1979   Ecology and Acculturation among Native Peoples of Central Brazil. *Science* 206:1043-50.

Gunn, J.
    1981   Traditional Agricultural Adaptation to Riverine Periodicity in the Amazon Basin. Research proposal.

Gupta, K. M. and M. Desai, eds.
    1979   *Man and Forest: A New Dimension in the Himalayas.* New Delhi: Today and Tomorrow's Printers and Publishers.

Hames, R. B.
    1979   Game Depletion and Hunting Zone Rotation Among the Yekuana and Yanomamo of Amazonas, Venezuela. Paper presented at the 43rd International Congress of Americanists, Vancouver, B.C.

1980a   Studies on Hunting and Fishing in the Neotropics. Working Papers on South American Indians, #2. Bennington, VT: Bennington College.

1980b   Monoculture, Polyculture, and Polyvariety in Tropical Forest Swidden Cultivation. Paper presented at the 79th Annual Meeting of the American Anthropological Association. 7 December. Washington, DC.

Hames, R. B. and W. T. Vickers
1982   Optimal Diet Breadth Theory as a Model to Explain Variability in Amazon Hunting. *American Ethnologist* 9(2):358-378.

Hammond, N.
1977   *Social Process in Maya Prehistory.* New York: Academic Press.

Hardwood, R. R.
1979   Small Farm Development: Understanding and Improving Farming Systems in the Humid Tropics. Boulder, CO.

Harris, D. R.
1971   The Ecology of Swidden Cultivation in the Upper Orinoco Rainforest, Venezuela. *The Geographical Review* 61(4):475-495.

1972   Swidden Systems and Settlement. In P. J. Ecko et al., eds. *Man, Settlement and Urbanism.* pp. 245-262. Cambridge, MA.

Harrison, P. D.
1978   *Pre-Hispanic Maya Agriculture.* Albuquerque: University of New Mexico Press.

Hart, J.
1979   Nomadic Hunters and Village Cultivators: A Study of Subsistence Interdependence in the Ituri Forest of Zaire. M.A. thesis, Department of Geography, Michigan State University.

Hart, R. D.
1980   A Natural Ecosystem Analog Approach to the Design of a Successional Crop System for Tropical Forest Environments. *Biotrópica* 12:73-83.

Hart, T. B. and J. A. Hart
1986   The Ecological Basis of Hunter-Gatherer Subsistence in African Rainforests: The Mbuti of Eastern Zaire. *Human Ecology* 14(1):29-55.

Hecht, S. B.
1981a   Deforestation in the Amazon Basin: Magnitude, Dynamics and Soil Resource Effects. In V. H. Sutlive, N. Altshuler and M. D. Zamora, eds. *Where Have All the Flowers Gone? Deforestation in the Third World.* Studies on Third World Societies, No.13. pp. 61-100. Williamsburg, VA: College of William and Mary.

1981b   Ecology and Agroforestry. *International Tree Crops Journal.*

1982a   Agroforestry in the Amazon Basin. In S. B. Hecht, ed. *Amazonia: Agriculture and Land Use Research.* pp. 331-372. Cali, Colombia: CIAT.

1982b   The Environmental Effect of Cattle Development in the Amazon Basin. Paper presented at the Conference on "Frontier Expansion in Amazonia," 8-11 February, Center for Latin American Studies, University of Florida, Gainesville.

Hecht, S. B. and D. A. Posey
1987   Management and Classification of Sociology the Kayapo Indians of Gorotire. In D. Posey and W. Balee, eds. *Resource Management by Caboclos and Indians in Amazonia.* New York: New York Botanical Gardens.

Herlihy, P.
1986   Indians and Rainforests Collide — The Cultural Parks of Darien. *Cultural Survival Quarterly* 10(3):57-61.

Hernandez, D. and A. J. Coutu
1981   Economic Evaluation of Slash/Burn Cultivation Options in Yurimaguas, Peru.

Agronomist Abstracts—American Society of Agronomists. 1981 Annual Meeting, Madison, Wisconsin.

Herrera, R.
1979   Nutrient Distribution and Cycling in an Amazon Caatinga Forest on Spodosols in Southern Venezuela. Ph.D. Dissertation, University of Reading, England.

Herrera, R. et al.
1978   Amazon Ecosystems: Their Structure and Functioning with Particular Emphasis on Nutrients. *Interciência* 3(4):223-31.

von Hildebrand, P.
1975   Observaciones preliminaries sobre utilización de tierras y fauna por los indígenas del río Mirití-Paraná. *Revista Colombiana de Antropología* 18:183-291.

Hiraoka, M.
1982   The Concept of Horizontal and Vertical Resource Use in Shifting Cultivation: The Case of Tamshiyacu, Peruvian Amazon. Paper presented at the meeting of the Conference of Latin Americanist Geographers, Santo Domingo, Dominican Republic.

Hodge, W. and D. Taylor
1957   Ethnobotany of the Island Caribs. *Webbia* 12:513-644.

Hoekstra, D. A.
1987   Economics of Agroforestry. *Agroforestry Systems* 5(3):293-300.

Hogbin, H. I. and P. Lawrence
1967   *Studies in New Guinea Land Tenure*. University Park: Pennsylvania State University Press.

Holmberg, A.
1969   *Nomads of the Long Bow*. New York: Natural History Press.

Horowitz, M. M.
1982   Notes on Training for Social and Community Forestry. Paper presented after USAID Community Forestry Workshop, 12-14 July, Washington, DC.

Hoskins, M. W.
1982a   Social Forestry in West Africa: Myths and Realities. Mimeo.

1982b   Observations on Indigenous and Modern Agroforestry Activities in West Africa. UNU, Workshop on Agroforestry, 31 May-5 June, Freiburg, West Germany.

1982c   Benefits Forgone as a Major Issue for FLCD Success. Paper presented at the USAID Community Forestry Workshop, 12-14 July, Washington, DC.

El Houri Ahmed, A.
1979   Effects of Land Use on Soil Characteristics in the Sudan. In H. O. Mongi and P. A. Huxley, eds. *Proceedings*. Expert Consultation on Soils Research in Agroforestry. pp. 1-13. Nairobi, Kenya: ICRAF.

Houseal, B. et al.
1985   Indigenous Cultures and Protected Areas in Central America. *Cultural Survival Quarterly* 9(1):10-20.

Huguet, L.
1978   Agroforestry, Proceedings of the US Strategy Conference on Tropical Deforestation. Washington, DC: US AID.

Hunn, E. S.
1975   A Measure of the Degree of Correspondence of Folk to Scientific Biological Classification. *American Ethnologist* 2(2):309-327.

1983   The Future of the World's Tropical Forests. *Commonwealth Forestry Review* 62(3):195-200.

Hunter, R. J.
1969   The Lack of Acceptance of the Pejibaye Palm and a Relative Comparison of Its Productivity to That of Maize. *Economic Botany* 23:237-245.

Huxley, P. A.
1979   Agroforestry Research: The Value of Existing Data Appraisal. In T. Chandler and D. Spurgeon, eds. *Proceedings*. Conference on International Cooperation in Agroforestry. pp. 297-315. Nairobi, Kenya: ICRAF.

1980a   Agroforestry at Degree Level: New Programme Structure. In T. Chandler and D. Spurgeon, eds. *International Cooperation in Agroforestry*. Nairobi, Kenya: ICRAF/DSE.

1980b   Research for the Development of Agroforestry Land-Use Systems. Paper presented at a research conference in Juba, Sudan, 2-6 June.

1982a   Agroforestry — A Range of New Opportunities. *Biologist* 29:141-143.

1982b   Developing Research for Agroforestry. *Span* 25:82-84.

1985   Experimental Agroforestry — Progress Through Perception and Collaboration. *Agroforestry Systems* 3(2):129-138.

1987   Agroforestry Experimentation: Separating the Wood from the Trees. *Agroforestry Systems* 5(3):251-275.

Huxley, P. A., ed.
1981   Plant Research and Agroforestry. Proceedings of a Consultative Meeting, 8-15 April. Nairobi, Kenya: ICRAF. 2 volumes.

Hyndman, D. C.
1982   Biotype Gradient in a Diversified New Guinea Subsistence System. *Human Ecology* 10:219-259.

Ibarra, R. A.
1979   Cultural-Ecological Adaptations to Black, White, and Blue Water Rivers in Amazonia: A Preliminary Study. *El Dorado* 4(1):1-27.

ICRAF
1982   *A Selected Bibliography on Agroforestry*. Nairobi, Kenya: ICRAF.

Igbozurike, M. U.
1971   Ecological Balance in Tropical Agriculture. *Geographical Review* 61(4):519-529.

1981   The Concept of Carrying-Capacity. *Journal of Geography* 80(4):141-149.

Innes, R. R.
1965   The Concept of the Woody Pasture in Low-Altitude Tropical Tree Savanna Environments. *IX International Grasslands Congress Proceedings* 2:1419-23.

IUCN (International Union for the Conservation of Nature)
1975   *The Use of Ecological Guidelines for Development in Tropical Forest Areas of South East Asia*.

1977   *Ecological Guidelines for Development in Tropical Rain Forests*.

Ives, J. D., S. Sabahasri and P. Voraurai
1978   Conservation and Development in Northern Thailand. Workshop paper on Agroforestry and Highland-Lowland Interactive Systems, 13-17 November, Chiang Mai University, Thailand.

Iyamabo, D. E.
1979   Ecological Aspects of Agroforestry in the Lowland Humid Tropics: West Africa. In T. Chandler and D. Spurgeon, eds. *Proceedings*. Conference on International Cooperation in Agroforestry. pp. 129-143. Nairobi, Kenya: ICRAF.

Janka, H.
1981   *Alternativas para el uso del suelo en áreas forestales del trópico humedo*. Mex-

ico City: Instituto Nacional de Investigaciones Forestales, Secretarias de
Agricultura y Recursos Hidráulicos.

Janzen, D. H.
1973   Tropical Agroecosystems. *Science* 182:1212-19.

1975   Tropical Agroecosystems. In P. Abelson, ed. *Food: Politics, Economics, ·Nutrition and Research.* Washington, DC: American Association for the Advancement of Science.

1986   Regrowing a Dry Tropical Forest. *News and Comment* 14:809.

Joergensen, A. B.
1977   Forest People in a World in Expansion. In C. Sandbacka, ed. *Cultural Imperialism and Cultural Identity.* pp. 77-96. Helsinki, Finland.

Johannessen, C. L.
1966   Pejibaye Palm: Yields Prices and Later Costs. *Economic Botany* 20(3):302-315.

Johnson, A.
1980   Ethnoecology and Planting Practices in a Swidden Agricultural System. In D. W. Brokensha et al., eds. *Indigenous Knowledge Systems and Development.* Washington, DC: University Press of America.

Johnson, D. V.
1983   Multi-Purpose Palms in Agroforestry: A Classification and Assessment. *International Tree Crops Journal* 2:217-244.

Jordan, C. F. and C. Uhl
1981   Nutrient Dynamics of Slash and Burn Agriculture in the Amazon Basin. Athens, GA: Institute of Ecology.

Junk, W. J.
1970   Investigations on the Ecology and Production Biology of the Floating Meadows on the Middle Amazon. *Amazoniana* 2:449-495.

1975   Aquatic Wild Life in Fisheries. In *The Use of Ecological Guidelines for Development in the American Humid Tropics.* Morges, Switzerland: IUCN.

Kazmi, S. M. A.
1979   *Yicib — Cordeauxia edulis Hems 1*: An Important Indigenous Plant of Somalia Which Has Many Uses. *Somalia Range Bulletin* 7:13-17.

Kellman, M. C.
1969   Some Environmental Components of Shifting Cultivation in Upland Mindanao. *Journal of Tropical Geography* 28:40-56.

Kellogg, C. E.
1963   Shifting Cultivation. *Soil Science* 95:221-230.

Kelly, R. D.
1977   The Significance of the Woody Component of Semi-Arid Savanna Vegetation in Relation to Meat Production. *Proceedings of the Grassland Society of South Africa* 12:105-108.

Kerr, W. E. and D. A. Posey
1984   Nova informacão sobre a agricultura dos Kayapó. *Interciência* 9(6):392-400.

Kerr, W. E., D. A. Posey and W. W. Filho
1978   Cupa, ou cipa babao, alimento de alguns índios amazônicas. *Acta Amazônica* 8(4):702-705.

King, K. F. S.
1968   Agri-Silviculture (The Taungya System). Bulletin 1. Department of Forestry, University of Ibadan, Nigeria.

1979a   Agroforestry and Fragile Ecosystems: Opening Address. In T. Chandler and D.

Spurgeon, eds. *Proceedings*. Expert Consultation on Soils Research in Agroforestry. pp. xxi-xxix. Nairobi, Kenya: ICRAF.

1979b   Concepts of Agroforestry. In T. Chandler and D. Spurgeon, eds. *Proceedings*. Conference on International Cooperation in Agroforestry. pp. 1-13. Nairobi, Kenya: ICRAF.

1979c   Agroforestry: A New System of Land Management. In *Symposium on Tropical Agriculture, 50th Proceedings* 303:1-10. Amsterdam: Royal Tropical Institute.

1979d   Agroforestry and the Utilization of Fragile Ecosystems. *Forest Ecology Management* 2:161-168.

King, K. F. S. and M. T. Chandler
1978   *The Wasted Lands: The Program of Work of the ICRAF*. Nairobi, Kenya: ICRAF.

Kio, P. R. Q.
1972   Shifting Cultivation and Multiple Use of Forest Land in Nigeria. *Commonwealth Forestry Review* 51(148):144-148.

Kirby, J.
1976   Agricultural Land-Use and the Settlement of Amazonia. *Pacific Viewpoint* 17:105-132.

Klee, G. A., ed.
1980   *World Systems of Traditional Resource Management*. New York: Halsted Press.

Kloos, P.
1971   *The Maroni River Caribs of Surinam*. Assen, Netherlands: Royal Van Gorcum and Co.

Kolawole, M. I.
1974   An Economic Assessment of Mixed Farming Systems in the Savanna Zone of Western Nigeria. *Nigerian Agricultural Journal* 11(2):133-142.

Krieg, M. B.
1964   *Green Medicine; The Search for Plants that Heal*. Chicago: Rand McNally.

Kunstadter, P. E., C. Chapman and S. Sabahasri, eds.
1978   *Farmers in the Forest: Economic Development and Marginal Agriculture in Northern Thailand*. Honolulu: Hawaii University Press.

La Font, P. B.
1959   The "slash-and-burn" (RAY) Agricultural System of the Mountain Populations of Central Vietnam. *Proceedings of the 9th Pacific Congress, 1957, Bangkok* 7:56-59.

Lagemann, J.
1977   Traditional African Farming in Eastern Nigeria: An Analysis of Reaction to Increasing Population Pressure. *Afrika Studien* 98:1-28. Verlag Munchen.

Lal, R.
1979   Effects of Cultural and Harvesting Practices on Soil Physical Conditions. In H. O. Mongi and P. A. Huxley, eds. *Proceedings*. Conference on Expert Consultation on Soils Research in Agroforestry. pp. 105-117. Nairobi, Kenya: ICRAF.

Lathrap, D.
1968a   Aboriginal Occupation and Changes in River Channel of the Central Ucayali, Peru. *American Antiquity* 33:62-79.

1968b   The Hunting Economies of the Tropical Rain Forest Zone of South America: An Attempt at a Historical Perspective. In R. B. Lee and I. DeVore, eds. *Man the Hunter*. Chicago: Aldine.

1970   *The Upper Amazon.* New York: Praeger.

1976   Our Father the Cayman, Our Mother the Gourd. In C. A. Reed, ed. *Origins of Agriculture.* The Hague: Mouton.

Leeds, A.
1961   Yaruro Incipient Tropical Forest Horticulture: Possibilities and Limits. In J. Wilbert, ed. *The Evolution of Horticultural Systems in Native South America: Causes and Consequences.* A Symposium. Supplement No. 2. pp. 13-46. Caracas, Venezuela: Antropologica.

Leguizamo, A.
1979   Ongoing Agroforestry in the Bajo Calima, Buenaventura. In T. Chandler and D. Spurgeon, eds. *Proceedings.* Conference on International Cooperation in Agroforestry. pp. 130-134. Nairobi, Kenya: ICRAF.

Leigh, J. H., A. D. Wilson and W. E. Mulham
1978   Seasonal Variations in the Leaf Fall and Quality of the Leaves of Four Australian Fodder Trees. *Australian Rangeland Journal* 1(2):137-141.

Leon, L.
1984   Project Reports—A Carpentry Workshop for the Huichol. *Cultural Survival Quarterly* 8(3):70-71.

Linares, O. F.
1976   "Garden Hunting" in the American Tropics. *Human Ecology* 4(4):331-349.

Lipp, F.
1971   Ethnobotany of the Chimantec Indians, Oaxaca, Mexico. *Economic Botany* 25:234-244.

Lojan, L.
1979   Agroforestry in Southern Ecuador. In T. Chandler and D. Spurgeon, eds. *Proceedings.* Conference on International Cooperation in Agroforestry. pp. 127-129. Nairobi, Kenya: ICRAF.

Loucks, O. L.
1980   Emergence of Research on Agro-Ecosystems. *Annual Review of Ecological Systems* 8:173-192.

Lovejoy, T. E. and H. D. R. Schubert
1980   The Ecology of Amazonian Development. In F. Barbira-Scazzocchio, ed. *Land, People and Planning in Contemporary Amazonia.* pp. 21-26. Cambridge: Cambridge University Press.

Lundgren, B.
1985   Global Deforestation, Its Causes and Suggested Remedies. *Agroforestry Systems* 3(2):91-95.

Lundgren, B. and J. B. Raintree
1983   Sustained Agroforestry. In *Agricultural Research for Development: Potentials and Challenges in Asia.* The Hague: ISNAR.

McDonald, D. R.
1977   Food Taboos: A Primitive Environmental Protection Agency (South America). *Anthropos* 72:734-748.

Macdonald, Jr., T.
1982   Report Submitted to the [USAID] Community Forestry Workshop, 12-14 July, Washington, DC.

1986   Anticipating *Colonos* and Cattle in Ecuador and Colombia. *Cultural Survival Quarterly* 10(2):33-36.

Macdonald, Jr., T., ed.
1985   *Native Peoples and Economic Development: Six Case Studies from Latin America.* Cultural Survival Report No. 16. Cambridge, MA: Cultural Survival.

McNeely, J. A. and K. R. Miller
    1984   *National Parks, Conservation and Development: The Role of Protected Areas in Sustaining Society.* Proceedings of the World Congress on National Parks, 11-12 October 1982, Bali, Indonesia. Washington, DC: Smithsonian Institution Press.

Maier, E.
    1979   *La Chinampa Tropical.* Mexico City: Centro de Ecodesarrollo.

Maimo, A.
    1979   Agro-Forestry Project Cameroon: Report of Progress for Period May 1977 to November 1979. Yaounde, Cameroon: ONAREST. Mimeo.

Manners, H. I.
    1981   Ecological Succession in New and Old Swiddens of Montane Papua New Guinea. *Human Ecology* 9(3):359-377.

Martin, F. W. and R. M. Ruberte
    1978   Wild Animals and Plants as Sources of Food. In F. W. Martin and R. M. Ruberte, eds. *Survival and Subsistence in the Tropics.* pp. 105-117. Antillian College, Mayaguez, Puerto Rico.

Mary, F. and G. Michon
    1987   When Agroforests Drive Back Natural Forests: A Socio-Economic Analysis of a Rice-Agroforest System in Sumatra. *Agroforestry Systems* 5(1):27-55.

Massing, A.
    1979   Economic Development and Its Effect on Traditional Land Use Systems in the Tropical Forests of West Africa. *Studies in Third World Societies* 8:73-95.

Masson, A. and J. Bersez
    1976   *La medicine d'Asklepios: Essais sur les connaissances anciennes.* 2nd ed. Paris: Imp. Bersez-Lug.

Maxwell, T. J. et al.
    1979   Integration of Forestry and Agriculture: A Model. *Agricultural Systems* 4(3):161-187.

May, P. H. et al.
    1985a   Subsistence Benefits from the Babassu Palm (*Orbignya martiana*). *Economic Botany* 39(2):113-129.

    1985b   Babassu Palm in the Agroforestry Systems in Brazil's Mid-North Region. *Agroforestry Systems* 3(3):275-295.

von Maydell, H. J.
    1979   The Development of Agroforestry in the Sahelian Zone of Africa. In T. Chandler and D. Spurgeon, eds. *Proceedings.* Conference on International Cooperation in Agroforestry. Nairobi, Kenya: ICRAF.

    1985   The Contribution of Agroforestry to World Forestry Development. *Agroforestry Systems* 3(2):83-90.

    1987   Editorial: International Research in Agroforestry. *Agroforestry Systems* 5(3): 193-195.

Mburu, O. M.
    1981   Agroforestry in Forest Management in Kenya. In L. Buck, ed. *Proceedings.* Kenya National Seminar on Agroforestry. pp. 19-22. Nairobi, Kenya: ICRAF.

Mecha, I. and T. A. Agdebola
    1980   Chemical Composition of Some Southern Nigeria Forage Eaten by Goats. International Symposium on Browse in Africa. Addis Ababa: ILCA.

Meggers, B.
    1954   Environmental Limitations on the Development of Culture. *American Anthropologist* 56:801-824.

1971   *Amazonia: Man and Culture in a Counterfeit Paradise*. Chicago: Aldine.

Meggers, B., E. S. Ayensu and W. D. Duckworth
1973   *Tropical Forest Ecosystems in Africa and South America: A Comparative Review*. Washington, DC: Smithsonian Institution Press.

Mergen, F.
1987   Research Opportunities to Improve the Production of Homegardens. *Agroforestry Systems* 5(1):57-67.

Messer, E.
1978   Zapotec Plant Knowledge: Classification, Uses and Communication about Plants in Mitka, Oaxaca, Mexico. Memoirs. Museum of Anthropology 5(1) part 2. Ann Arbor: University of Michigan.

Metzner, H.
1981   Innovations in Agriculture Incorporating Traditional Production Methods: The Case of Amarasi (Timor). *Applied Geography and Development* 17:91-107.

Michaelson, T.
1980   Ordenación integrada de cuencas hidrográficas: la estrategia de un proyecto en Honduras. Tegucigalpa, Honduras: CHDF.

Miracle, M.
1967   *Agriculture in the Congo Basin*. Madison: University of Wisconsin Press.

Mongi, H. O. and P. A. Huxley, eds.
1979   *Soils Research in Agroforestry*. Nairobi, Kenya: ICRAF.

Montague, P.
1981   His "Crop" Is Crocodiles. *International Wildlife* 11(2):21-28.

Moran, E. F.
1974   The Adaptive System of the Amazonian *Caboclo*. In C. Wagley, ed. *Man in the Amazon*. pp. 136-159. Gainesville: University of Florida Press.

1976   Manioc Deserves More Recognition in Tropical Farming. *World Crops* (UK) 28(4):184.

1979a   An Energetics View of Manioc Cultivation in the Amazon. In D. L. Browman and R. A. Schwartz, eds. *Peasants, Primitives and Proletariats—The Struggle for Identity in South America*. pp. 111-123. The Hague: Mouton.

1979b   Stratégies for Survival: Resource-Use Along the Transamazon Highway. *Studies in Third World Societies* 7:49-75.

1981   *Developing the Amazon*. Bloomington: Indiana University Press.

1982a   Ecological, Anthropological, and Agronomic Research in the Amazon Basin. *Latin American Research Review* 17(1):3-41.

1982b   *The Dilemma of Amazonian Development*. Boulder: University of Colorado Press.

Moran, K.
1987   Traditional Elephant Management in Sri Lanka. *Cultural Survival Quarterly* 11(1):23-26.

Morauta, L. et al., eds.
1980   *Traditional Conservation in Papua New Guinea*. Boroko, Papua New Guinea: Institute of Applied Social and Economic Research.

Morgan, W. B.
1955   Farming Practice, Settlement Pattern and Population Density in Southeastern Nigeria. *Geographical Journal* 121:320-333.

Moss, R. P.
1968   *The Soil Resource of Tropical Africa*. Cambridge: Cambridge University Press.

Mouttapa, F.
1974   Soil Aspects in the Practice of Shifting Cultivation in Africa and the Need for a Common Approach to Soil and Land Resources. In FAO Shifting Cultivation and Soil Conservation in Africa. *FAO Soils Bulletin* 24:37-41.

Murphy, R. and Y. Murphy
1974   *Women of the Forest*. New York: Columbia University Press.

Myers, N.
1979   *The Sinking Ark*. Oxford: Pergamon Press.

1981   Deforestation in the Tropics: Who Wins, Who Loses? In U. G. Sutlive, N. Altshuler and M. D. Zamora, eds. *Where Have All the Flowers Gone? Deforestation in the Third World*. Studies in Third World Societies No.13. pp. 1-24. Williamsburg, VA: College of William and Mary.

1983   *A Wealth of Wild Species: Storehouse for Human Welfare*. Boulder, CO: Westview Press.

Nabhan, G. P. and T. E. Sheridan
1977   Living Fence Rows of the Rio San Miguel, Sonora, Mexico: Traditional Technology for Flood/Plain Management. *Human Ecology* 5:97-111.

Nair, P. K. R.
1979   Agroforestry Research: A Retrospective and Prospective Appraisal. In T. Chandler and D. Spurgeon, eds. *Proceedings*. Conference on International Cooperation in Agroforestry. pp. 275-296. Nairobi, Kenya: ICRAF.

1982a   *Soil Productivity Aspects of Agroforestry*. Nairobi, Kenya: ICRAF.

1982b   Tree Integration on Farmlands for Sustained Productivity of Smallholdings. Paper presented at 4th International Conference on Resource-Conserving, Environmentally Sound Agricultural Alternatives at MIT, Cambridge, MA.

1983a   Multiple Land Use and Agroforestry. In *Better Crops for Food*. CIBA Foundation Symposium 97. pp. 101-115. London: Pitman Books Ltd.

1983b   Some Promising Agroforestry Technologies for Hilly and Semi-Arid Regions of Rwanda. Paper given at the Rwanda/ISNAR seminar on Agricultural Research in Rwanda, 5-12 February, Kigali, Rwanda.

1983c   Tree Integration on Farmlands for Sustained Productivity of Small Holdings. Paper presented at the 14th International Conference of IFOAM at MIT, August 1982, Cambridge, MA.

1985   Classification of Agroforestry Systems. *Agroforestry Systems* 3(2):97-128.

1987   Agroforestry Systems Inventory. *Agroforestry Systems* 5(3):301-317.

Nair, P. K. R. et al.
1984   Agroforestry as an Alternative to Shifting Cultivation. Paper presented at the Expert Consultation on Alternatives to Shifting Cultivation, 22-25 February, Rome. Proceedings in press.

National Academy of Sciences
1975   *Underexploited Tropical Plants with Promising Economic Value*. Washington, DC: National Academy of Sciences.

1980   *Research Priorities in Tropical Biology*. Washington, DC: National Academy of Sciences.

National Research Council (US)
1982   *Ecological Aspects of Development in the Humid Tropics*. Washington, DC: National Academy Press.

National Research Council/National Academy of Sciences
1980   *Conversion of Tropical Moist Forests*. Washington, DC: NRC/NAS.

Nations, J. D.
   1981   The Rainforest Farmers. *Pacific Discovery* January-February.

Nations, J. D. and D. I. Komer
   1983   Central America's Tropical Rain Forest: Positive Steps for Survival. *Ambio* 12(5):232-238.

Nations, J. D. and R. B. Nigh
   1978   Cattle, Cash, Food and Forest: The Destruction of the American Tropics and the Lacandon Maya Alternative. *Culture and Agriculture* 6:15.

   1980   The Evolutionary Potential of Lacandon Maya Sustained Yield Tropical Forest Agriculture. *Journal of Anthropological Research* 36(1):1-30.

New American Scientist
   1982   Issue on Destruction of the Amazon. July/August.

Nicholaides, J. J. et al.
   1982   Continuous Cropping Potential in the Amazon. Mimeo.

Nietschmann, B.
   1972   Hunting and Fishing Focus among the Miskito Indians of Eastern Nicaragua. *Human Ecology* 1:41-67.

   1973   *Between Land and Water: The Subsistence Ecology of the Miskito Indians, Eastern Nicaragua.* New York: Seminar Press.

Nigh, R. B. and J. D. Nations
   1980   Tropical Rainforests. *The Bulletin of the Atomic Scientists* 36(3):12-19.

Nimuendajú, C.
   1952   The Tapajo. *The Kroeber Anthropological Society* 6:1-25. Berkeley, CA.

   1974   Farming Among the Eastern Timbira. In P. J. Lyon, ed. *Native South Americans.* pp 111-119. Boston: Little Brown and Co.

Ninez, U. K.
   1984   Household Gardens: Theoretical Considerations on an Old Survival Strategy. Research series 1. Lima, Peru: International Potato Center.

Norgaard, R. B.
   1981   Sociosystem and ecosystem coevolution in the Amazon. *Journal of Environmental Economics and Management* 8(3):238-254.

Norman, M. J. T.
   1978   Energy Inputs and Outputs of Subsistence Systems in the Tropics. *Agro-Ecosystems* 4:355-366.

   1979   *Annual Cropping Systems in the Tropics: An Introduction.* Gainesville: University Presses of Florida.

Noronha, R.
   1980   Sociological Aspects of Forestry Project Design. Washington, DC: World Bank AGR Technical Note.

   1981   Traditional Land Tenures, Land Use Systems and the Design of Agricultural Projects (Draft). Washington, DC: The World Bank.

   1982   Seeing People for the Trees: Social Issues in Forestry. Mimeo.

Nova, A. and J. Posner
   1980   *Agricultura de Ladera en América Tropical.* Turrialba, Costa Rica: CATIE.

Nye, P. H.
   n.d.   Changes in the Soil After Clearing Tropical Forest. *Plant and Soil* 21(1):101-112.

Nye, P. H. and D. J. Greenland
   1960   *The Soil Under Shifting Cultivation.* Technical Communication #51. Harpender: Commonwealth Bureau of Soils. 156 pages.

Oduol, P. A.
1986   The Shamba System: An Indigenous System of Food Production from Forest Areas of Kenya. *Agroforestry Systems* 4(4):365-373.

Office of Technology Assessment, Congress of the United States
1984   *Technologies to Sustain Tropical Forest Resources.* Washington, DC: US Government Printing Office.

Okafor, J. C.
1980a   Tree for Food and Fodder in the Savanna Areas of Nigeria. *International Tree Crops Journal* 1(2/3):131-141.

1980b   Progress in the Selection and Improvement of Indigenous Edible Trees for Food Production and Agroforestry in the Nigerian Forest Zone. Paper presented at the IUFRO Symposium and Workshop on Genetics Improvement and Productivity of Fast-Growing Tree Species, Brazil.

Olofson, H.
1981   *Adaptive Strategies and Change in Philippine Swidden Based Societies.* Los Banos, Philippines: Forest Research Institute.

1983   Indigenous Agroforestry Systems. *Philippine Quarterly of Culture and Society* 11:149-174.

n.d.   An Anthropological Approach to Social Forestry: The Study of Indigenous Agroforestry Systems. Department of Social Forestry, University of the Philippines, Los Banos. Mimeo.

Openshaw, K. and J. Morris
1979   The Socio-Economics of Agro-Forestry. In T. Chandler and D. Spurgeon, eds. *Proceedings.* Conference on International Cooperation in Agroforestry. pp. 327-351. Nairobi, Kenya: ICRAF.

Oracion, T.
1963   Kaungin Agriculture Among the Bukidnond of Southeastern Negros, Philippines. *Tropical Geography* 17:213-224.

O'Riodan, T.
1971   *Perspectives on Resource Management.* London.

Ortiz Monasterio, R.
1950   Reconocimiento agrológico regional del estado de Yucatán. *Boletín de la Sociedąd Mexicana de Geografica y Estadística* 69:245-324.

Overal, W. L. and D. Posey
1987   Uso de formigas *Azteca* para controle biológico de pragos agrícolas entre os índios Kayapó. *Revista Brasileira Zoológica.*

Padoch, C. et al.
1985   Amazonian Agroforestry: A Market-Oriented System in Peru. *Agroforestry Systems* 3(1):47-58.

Padoch, C. and A. P. Vayda
1983   Patterns of Resource Use and Human Settlement in Tropical Forests. In F. B. Galley, ed. *Tropical Rainforest Ecosystems: Structure and Function.* Vol. 14A. Ecosystems of the World. Amsterdam: Elsevier.

Panday, K.
1975   Importance of Fodder Trees and Tree Fodder in Nepal. Post-graduate Diploma Thesis submitted to Prof. J. Noesberger, Institute of Plant Production, Federal Technical University, Zurich, Switzerland.

Pao Chan, K.
1977   Agro-forestry: Its Concepts Implication of a Sound Land-Use Goal. *Canopy* (Philippines) 3(11):6-7, 10.

Parker, E.
  1981   Cultural Ecology and Change: A *Caboclo* Varzea Community in the Brazilian
          Amazon. Ph.D. Dissertation, Department of Geography, University of Col-
          orado, Boulder.

  1983   Agriculture, Development and the Amazon Varzea: A Reappraisal. Unpublished
          manuscript.

Parker, E. et al.
  1983   Resource Exploitation in Amazonia: Ethnological Examples from Four Popula-
          tions. *Annals of Carnegie Museum* 52(Article 8)16 September. Pittsburgh:
          Carnegie Museum of Natural History.

Parmar, Y. S.
  1978   Food from Forest in Hilly Areas of India. Mimeo.

Parsons, J. J. and W. M. Denevan
  1967   Pre-Colombian Ridged Fields. *Scientific American* 217(1):92-100.

Patino, V. M.
  1963   *Plantas cultivadas y animales domésticas en América Equinoccial.* 6 volumes.
          Cali, Colombia: CIAT.

Peck, R. B.
  1979   Traditional Forestation of Local Farmers in the Tropics. In G. de las Salas, ed.
          Proceedings. Workshop on Agroforestry Systems in Latin America. Turrialba,
          Costa Rica: CATIE.

Pelzer, K. J.
  1978   Swidden Cultivation in Southeast Asia: Historical, Ecological and Economic
          Perspectives. In P. Kunstadter, E. C. Chapman and S. Sabahasri, eds. *Farmers
          in the Forest.* pp. 271-286. Honolulu: University Press of Hawaii.

Peterson, J.
  1978   Hunter-Gatherer/Farmer Exchange. *American Anthropologist* 80:335-351.

Phillips, R. E.
  1980   No Tillage Agriculture. *Science* 208:1100-13.

Phillips, J. F. V.
  1960   *Agriculture and Ecology in Africa, A Study of Actual and Potential Develop-
          ment South of the Sahara.* New York: Praeger.

  1966   *The Development of Agriculture and Forestry in the Tropics: Patterns, Prob-
          lems, and Promise.* 2nd ed. London.

Pimental, D., S. A. Levin and D. Olson
  1978   Coevolution and the Stability of Exploiter-Victim. *The American Naturalist*
          112(983):119-125.

Pires, J. M.
  1978   The Forest Ecosystems of the Brazilian Amazon: Description, Functioning and
          Research Needs. In UNESCO, ed. *Tropical Forest Ecosystems.* Paris: UNESCO.

Poblete, E. O.
  1969   *Plantas medicinales de Bolivia.* Cochabamba, Bolivia: Los Amigos del Libro.

Popenoe, H.
  1960   Effects of Shifting Cultivation on Natural Soil Constituents in Central America.
          Ph.D. dissertation, University of Florida (IFAS).

Poschen, P.
  1986   An Evaluation of the *Acacia albida*-Based Agroforestry Practices in the
          Hararghe Highlands of Eastern Ethiopia. *Agroforestry Systems* 4(2):129-143.

Posey, D. A.
  1978   Ethnoentomological Survey of Amerind Groups in Lowland Latin America. *The
          Florida Entomologist* 61(4):225-229.

1979   Kayapó controla inseto com uso adequado do ambiente. *Revista de Atualidade Indígena* 3(14):47-58.

1980   Algunes observaciones etnoentomologicas sobre grupos Amerindios en la America Latina. *America Indígena* 15(1):105-120.

1981   Ethnoentomology of the Kayapó Indians of Central Brazil. *Journal of Ethnobiology* 1(1):165-174.

1982a Nomadic Agriculture of the Amazon. *Garden* 6(1):18-24. New York: The New York Botanical Gardens.

1982b The Keepers of the Forest. *Garden* 6(1):18-24. New York: The New York Botanical Gardens.

1983a Indigenous Knowledge and Development: An Ideological Bridge to the Future. *Ciência e Cultura* 35(7):877-894.

1983b Indigenous Ecological Knowledge and Development of the Amazon. In E. Moran, ed. *The Dilemma of Amazonian Development*. pp. 225-257. Boulder, CO: Westview Press.

1983c Folk Apiculture of the Kayapó Indians of Brazil. *Biotropica* 15(2):154-158.

1984a Keepers of the Campo. *Garden* 8(6):8ff. New York: The New York Botanical Gardens.

1984b Os Kayapó e a natureza. *Ciência Hoje* 3(12):36-45.

1985   Indigenous Management of Tropical Forest Ecosystems: The Case of the Kayapó Indians of the Brazilian Amazon. *Agroforestry Systems* 3(2):139-158.

1986a Ethnoecology and the Investigation of Resource Management by the Kayapó Indians of Gorotire, Brazil. Paper given at a Symposium on Tropical Ecology. *Proceedings*. Belem, Brazil: EMBRAPA/CPATU.

1986b Manejo da floresta secundaria, capoeiras, campos e cerrados (Kayapó). In D. Ribeiro, ed. *Suma Etnológica Brasileira*. Vol. 1: Etnobiologia. Petropolis, Brasil: Vozes/FINEP.

1987a Folk Sciences and the Generation of New Management and Conservation Models for Amazonia. In D. Posey and W. Balee, eds. *Natural Resource Management by Indigenous and Folk Societies in Amazonia*. New York: The New York Botanical Gardens.

1987b Ethnoentomological Survey of Brazilian Indians. *Entomol. Gener.* 12(2/3): 191-202.

Posey, D. and W. Balee, eds.
in   *Natural Resource Management by Indigenous and Folk Societies in Amazonia*.
press New York: The New York Botanical Gardens.

Posey, D. A. et al.
1984   Ethnoecology as Applied Anthropology in Amazonian Development. *Human Organization* 43(2):95-107.

Prance, G. T. and A. E. Prance
1972   The Botany of a Brazilian Tribe. *Garden Journal* 22:132-142.

Prance, G. T., D. G. Campbell and B. W. Nelson
1977   The Ethnobotany of the Paumari Indians. *Economic Botany* 31(2): 129-139.

Pratchett, D. et al.
       Factors Limiting Liveweight Gain of Beef Cattle on Rangeland in Botswana. *Journal of Range Management* 30(6):442-445.

Prentice, W.
    1979   Rehabilitation of Exhausted Lands in the Upper Ecuadorian Amazon. In G. De
            las Salas, ed. *Proceedings*. Workshop on Agroforestry Systems in Latin
            America, Turrialba, Costa Rica. pp. 153-57. Turrialba, Costa Rica: CATIE.

Price, B. J.
    1971   Prehispanic Irrigation Agriculture in Nuclear America. *Latin American Research
            Review* 7(3):3-60.

Price, T. and L. Hall
    1983   Agricultural Development in the Mexican Tropics: Alternatives for the Selva
            Lacandona Region of Chiapas. Ithaca, NY: Department of Agriculture
            Economics, Cornell University.

Pritzker, A. S.
    1978   Ecological Effects of Mountain Slash and Burn Cultivation—A Study of the
            Mountain Kaingin Farming System (1975-1978). MAB Philippines, Manila.
            Mimeo.

    1981   Ecological Concerns of the Tropical Hemisphere: Environmental Aspects of
            Deforestation and Destruction. University of Maine at Orono. Mimeo.

Puleston, D.
    1968   *Brosium alicastrum* as a Subsistence Alternative for the Classic Maya of the
            Central Southern Lowlands. M.A. thesis, University of Pennsylvania.

    1971   An Experimental Approach to the Function of Classic Maya Chultuns. *American
            Antiquity* 36:322-335.

Raintree, J. B.
    n.d.   Readings for a Socially Relevant Agroforestry. Paper Presented at the
            ICRAF/DSE International Workshop on Professional Education in Agroforestry.
            Nairobi, Kenya: ICRAF.

    1983   Strategies for Enhancing the Adoptability of Agroforestry Innovations.
            Agroforestry Systems 1(3):173-188.

    1987   The State of the Art of Agroforestry Diagnosis and Design. *Agroforestry
            Systems* 5(3): 219-250.

Raintree, J. B. and K. Warner
    1986   Agroforestry Pathways for the Intensification of Shifting Cultivation.
            Agroforestry Systems 4(1):39-54.

Rappaport, R. A.
    1967   *Pigs for the Ancestors*. New Haven, CT: Yale University Press.

    1971   The Flow of Energy in an Agricultural Society. *Scientific American* 225.

Redford, K. H. and J. G. Robinson
    1985   Hunting by Indigenous Peoples and Conservation of Game Species. *Cultural
            Survival Quarterly* 9(1):41-44.

Reed, R. R.
    1965   Swidden in Southeast Asia. *Lipunan* 1(1):24.

Rees, J. D.
    1972   Forest Utilization by Tarascan Agriculturalists in Michoacan, Mexico. Disserta-
            tion Abstracts International B 32(11)6466-467.

Reichel-Dolmatoff, G.
    1974   *Amazonian Cosmos*. Chicago: University of Chicago Press.

    1976   Cosmology as Ecological Analysis: A View from the Rain Forest. *MAN*
            11(3):307-318.

    1978   Desana Animal Categories, Food Restrictions, and the Concept of Color
            Energies. *Journal of Latin American Lore* 4(2):243-291.

Richards, P. W.
1952   The Tropical Rain Forest. Cambridge: Cambridge University Press.

1969   Speciation in the Tropical Rain Forest and the Concept of the Niche. Biological Journal of the Linnaean Society 1:149-153.

1973   The Tropical Rain Forest. Scientific American 229:58-67.

Rivera Chavez, P. L.
1980   Procedimiento para determinar el requerimiento de tierras de una familia nativa sedentaria en la selva baja. El Hombre y la Cultura Andina III:204-208. Lima, Peru.

Romanini, C.
1978   Agricultura Tropical en Tierras Ganaderas. Mexico City: Centro de Ecodesarrollo and Instituto Nacional Indigenista.

Romanoff, S.
1977   Informe sobre el uso de la tierra por los Matses en la selva baja peruana. Amazonia Peruana 1(1):97-132.

Roosevelt, A.C.
1980   Parmana: Prehistoric Maize and Manioc Subsistence along the Amazon and Orinoco. New York: Academic Press.

Ross, E. B.
1976   The Achuara Jivaro: Cultural Adaptation in the Upper Amazon. Ph.D. dissertation, Columbia University, New York.

1978a   The Evolution of the Amazon Peasantry. Journal of Latin American Studies 10:193-218.

1978b   Food Taboos, Diet and Hunting Strategy: The Adaptation to Animals in the Amazon Cultural Ecology. Current Anthropology 19(1):1-36.

Royal Tropical Institute (RTI)
1979   Agroforestry: Proceedings of the 50th Tropiche Landbouwdag. Bulletin 303. Amsterdam: Department of Agricultural Research, RTI.

Ruddle, K.
1973   The Human Use of Insects: Examples from the Yupka. Biotrôpica 5(2):94-101.

1974   The Yupka Cultivation System: A Study of Shifting Cultivation in Colombia and Venezuela. Berkeley: University of California Press.

Ruthenberg, H.
1971   Systems with Perennial Crops. In H. Ruthenberg. Farming Systems in the Tropics. pp. 189-251. London: Oxford University Press.

Saffirio, J. et al.
1983   The Impact of Contact: Two Yanomamo Case Studies. Cultural Survival Occasional Paper No. 11 and Working Papers on South American Indians No. 6. Cambridge, MA: Cultural Survival.

de las Salas, G., ed.
1979   Workshop: Agroforestry Systems in Latin America. Turrialba, Costa Rica: CATIE.

Salick, J.
1987   Ethnobotany of the Amuesha Palcasu Valley, Peru. New York: The Institute of Economic Botany, The New York Botanical Gardens. Report produced for US AID. Grant No. 527-0166-G-00-4047-00.

Sanchez, P. A.
1972   Soil Management Under Shifting Cultivation. In Review of Soils Research in Tropical Latin America. pp. 62-64. North Carolina State University.

Sanchez, P. A. and M. A. Nurena
1970   Upland Rice Improvement Under Shifting Cultivation Systems in the Amazon Basin of Peru. Paper presented at the 1970 IRRI Conference, Los Banos, the Philippines. Mimeo.

1974   Investigaciones en manejo de suelos tropicales en Yurimaguas, selva baja del Peru. Paper presented at the Seminario de Sistemas de Agricultura Tropical, June 1974, Lima, Peru.

1980   Soils in the Humid Tropics. *Studies in Third World Societies* 14:347-410.

de Schlippe, P.
1956   *Shifting Cultivation in Africa: The Zande System of Agriculture.* London: Routledge & Kegan Paul.

Schmink, M. and C. H. Wood, eds.
1984   *Frontier Expansion in Amazonia.* Gainesville: University of Florida Press.

Schwartzman, S.
1986   *Seringueiros* Defend the Rainforest in Amazonia. *Cultural Survival Quarterly* 10(2):41-43.

Scott, G.
1974   Effects of Shifting Cultivation in the Gran Pajonal, Eastern Peru. *Annals of the Association of American Geographers* 6:58-61.

Sedjo, R. A. and M. Clawson
1983   How Serious Is Tropical Deforestation? *Journal of Forestry* 81(12):792-794.

Seeger, A.
1981   *Nature and Society in Central Brazil: The Suyá Indians of Mato Grosso.* Cambridge: Harvard University Press.

Seubert, C. E. et al.
1977   Effects of Land Clearing Methods on Soil Properties of an Ultisol and Crop Performance in the Amazon Jungle of Peru. *Tropical Agriculture* 54(4):307-321. Trinidad.

Shah, S. A.
n.d.   Social Forestry in the Life and Service of Indian People. Mimeo.

Sherman, D. G.
1980   The Culture-Bound Notion of 'Soil Fertility': On Interpreting Non-Western Criteria of Selecting Land for Cultivation. *Studies in Third World Societies* 14:487-511.

Sholes, R.
1984   The Irulu Snake Catcher Cooperative. *Cultural Survival Quarterly* 8(3):21-23.

Siemens, A. H. and D. E. Puleston
1972   Ridged Fields and Associated Features in Southern Campeche — New Perspectives on Lowland Maps. *American Antiquity* 37(2):228-239.

Singh, B. N. and B. P. Singh
1977   The Biotic Disturbance and Soil and Water Loss. *Indian Farming* 26(11):47-49.

Sioli, H.
1951   Alguns resultados e problemas da limnologia Amazônica. *Boletín Têcnico do Instituto Agronômico do Norte* No. 24. Belem, Brazil: IAN.

1973   Recent Human Activities in the Brazilian Amazon Region and Their Ecological Effects. In B. Meggers et al., eds. *Tropical Forest Ecosystems in Africa and South America.* Washington, DC: Smithsonian Institution.

1980   Forseeable Consequences of Actual Development Schemes and Alternative Ideas. In F. Barbira-Scazzocchio, ed. *Land, People and Planning in Contemporary Amazonia.* pp. 257-268. Cambridge: Cambridge University Press.

Siskind, J.
1973   *To Hunt in the Morning*. London: Oxford University Press.

Siverts, H.
1977   The Impact of Peruvian Expansion on Aguaruna Traditional Adaptation. In C.
Sandbacka, ed. *Cultural Imperialism and Cultural Identity*. pp. 37-48. Helsinki.

Smith, N. J. H.
1974   Destructive Exploitation of the South American River Turtle. In *Yearbook of
the Association of Pacific Coast Geographers* 36(c). Oregon State University
Press.

1977   Human Exploitation of Terra Firma Fauna in Amazonia. *Ciência e Cultura*
30(1):17-23.

1981a   *Man, Fisher, and the Amazon*. New York: Columbia University Press.

1981b   Colonization Lessons from a Tropical Forest. *Science* 214(4522):755-761.

1982   *Rainforest Corridors: The Transamazon Colonization Scheme*. Berkeley:
University of California Press.

Smith, R. C.
1987   Indigenous Autonomy for Grassroots Development. *Cultural Survival Quarterly*
11(1):8-12.

Smole, W. J.
1976   *The Yanomamo Indians: A Cultural Geography*. Austin: University of Texas
Press.

Social Ecology of the Amazon
1979   University of Illinois, Urbana. 2 vols. Collection of photocopies.

Spencer, J. E.
1966   *Shifting Cultivation in Southeast Asia*. Publications in Geography No. 19.
Berkeley: University of California Press.

Spurgeon, D.
1979a   Agroforestry: New Hope for Subsistence Farmers. *Nature* 280:533-534.

1979b   Growing Food in the Forests. *Uniterra* 4(6):4-5.

1980   Agroforestry: A Promising System of Improved Land Management for Latin
America. *Interciência* 5:176-178.

Srivastava, B. P.
1979   Ecological Aspects of Agroforestry in Mountainous Zones: The Himalayan
Region. In T. Chandler and D. Spurgeon, eds. *Proceedings*. Conference on International Cooperation in Agroforestry. pp. 53-67. Nairobi, Kenya: ICRAF.

Stark, N.
1969   Direct Nutrient Cycling in the Amazon Basin. In *Il Simposio y Foro de Biologia
Tropical Amazonica*. Bogota, Colombia: Editorial Pax.

1971   Nutrient Cycling. *Tropical Ecology* 12(1):24-50.

Steggerda, M.
1941   *Maya Indians of Yucatan*. Publication No. 531. Washington, DC: Carnegie
Institute.

Steinlin, H.
1979   Development of New Agro-Forestry Land Use Systems in the Humid Tropics.
Plant Research and Development 10:7-17.

Sternberg, H. O'R.
1973   Development and Conservation. *Erdkunde* 23:253-265.

Stevens, R. L.
  1964   The Soils of Middle America and Their Relation to Indian Peoples and Cultures. In R. Wauchope, ed. *Handbook of Middle American Indians* 1:265-315. Austin: University of Texas Press.

Stocks, A.
  1980   Candoshi and Cocamilla Swiddens in Eastern Peru. Paper presented at the 79th Annual Meeting of the American Anthropological Association, 7 December, Washington, DC.

Stromgaard, P.
  1984a   Field Studies of Land Use Under Chitemene Shifting Cultivation, Zambia. *Geografisk Tidsskrift* 84:78-85.

  1984b   The Immediate Effects of Burning and Ash-Fertilization. *Plant and Soil* 80:307-320.

  1984c   Prospects of Improved Farming Systems in a Shifting Cultivation Area in Zambia. *Quarterly Journal of International Agriculture* 23(1):38-50.

  1985   A Subsistence Society Under Pressure: The Bemba of Northern Zambia. *Africa* 55(1):39-59.

Surujbally, R. S.
  1977   Game Farming Is a Reality. *Unasulva* 29(116):13-15.

Svanqvist, N.
  1976   *Employment Opportunities in the Tropical Moist Forest Under Alternative Silvicultural Systems, Including Agrisilvicultural Techniques.* Rome: FAO.

Synnott, T. J. et al.
  1976   The Relative Merits of Natural Regeneration Enrichment Planting, and Conversion Planting in Tropical Moist Forests, Including Agrisilvicultural Techniques. Rome: FAO. 12 pages.

Taylor, K.
  1975   *Sanuma Fauna: Prohibitions and Classifications.* Caracas, Venezuela: Fundacion La Salle de Ciências Naturales, Instituto Caribe de Antropologia y Sociologia.

Thangam, E. S.
  1977   Containing Shifting Cultivation. *Indian Farming* 26(11):55-56.

  1979   Shifting Cultivation in Aruachal Pradesh. Paper presented at seminar on agroforestry, Imphal, India.

Therez, D.
  1979   The Heritage and Creativity of Popular Ecological Knowledge as Underused Resources for Development. *Ecodevelopment News* 10(8):8-31.

Torres, F.
  1983   Agroforestry – Concepts and Practices. In D. Hoekstra and F. M. Kuguru, eds. *Agroforestry Systems Small-Scale Farmers.* Nairobi, Kenya: ICRAF/BAT.

Torres-Trueba, H. E.
  1968   Slash-and-Burn Cultivation in the Tropical Forest Amazon: Its Technoenvironmental Limitations and Potentialities for Cultural Development. *Sociologus* 18(2):137-151. Berlin.

Tosi, J. A. and R. F. Voertman
  1964   Some Environmental Factors in the Economic Development of the Tropics. *Economic Geography* 4(3):189-205.

Townsend, J.
   1982   Seasonality and Capitalist Penetration in the Amazon Basin. Paper presented at
          Change in the Amazon Basin, 44th Congress of Americanists, September,
          Manchester.

Tracey, J.
   1982   Bora Indian Agro-Forestry: An Alternative to Deforestation. *Cultural Survival
          Quarterly* 6(2):15-16.

Turner II, B. L.
   1974   Prehistoric Intensive Agriculture in the Mayan Lowlands. *Science* 185:118-124.

   1977   Intensive Agriculture Among the Highland Tzeltal. *Ethnology* 16(2):167-174.

Turner II, B. L., R. Q. Hannam and A. V. Portavovo
   1977   Population Pressure and Agricultural Intensity. *Annals of the Association of
          American Geographers* 67:384-396.

Uhl, C.
   1980   Studies of Forest Agricultural and Successional Environments in the Upper Rio
          Negro Region of the Amazon Basin. Ph.D. dissertation, Michigan State
          University.

   1983   You Can Keep a Good Forest Down. *Natural History* 92(4):69-79.

Uhl, C. et al.
   1981   Early Plant Succession After Cutting and Burning in the Upper Rio Negro
          Region of the Amazon Basin. *Journal of Ecology* 69:631-649.

Uhl, C. and P. Murphy
   1981   A Comparison of Productivities and Energy Values Between Slash-and-Burn
          Agriculture and Secondary Succession in the Upper Rio Negro Region of the
          Amazon, Brazil. *Agro-systems* 7(1):63-83.

   1982   Traditional and Innovative Approaches to Agriculture on Amazon Basin Ox-
          isols. In R. Todd, ed. *Nutrient Cycling in Agroecosystems*. London.

UNEP
   1980   *Overview Document: Experts Meeting on Tropical Forests Ecosystems.* Ven-
          dome, France: UNESCO.

   1982   The Global Assessment of Tropical Forest Resources. Gems Pac Information
          Series No. 3. Nairobi, Kenya: UNEP/FAO.

UNESCO
   1978a *Tropical Forest Ecosystems: A State of Knowledge Report.* Paris: UNESCO.

   1978b Management of Natural Resources in Africa: Traditional Strategies and Modern
          Decision Making. MAB. Technical Notes #9. Paris: UNESCO.

UPCF
   1964   Recommendations of the National Conference on the Kaingin Problem. UP Col-
          lege of Forestry, Laguna.

Upton, M.
   1973   *Farm Management in Africa — The Principles of Production and Planning.* Lon-
          don: Oxford University Press.

Uquillas, J. E.
   1985   Indian Land and Rights and National Resource Management in the Ecuadorian
          Amazon. In T. Macdonald, Jr., ed. *Native People and Economic Development:
          Six Case Studies from Latin America.* Cultural Survival Report No. 16. pp.
          87-98. Cambridge, MA: Cultural Survival.

US House of Representatives
   1981   *Tropical Deforestation: Hearings Before the Subcommittee on International
          Organizations of the Committee on Foreign Affairs — House of Representatives.*
          96th Congress, 2nd session (1980), Washington, DC.

US Interagency Task Force on Tropical Forests
1980   *The World's Tropical Forests: A Policy, Strategy and Program for the US.*
Washington, DC.

Van Nao, T.
1979   Activities of FAO in the Agroforestry Field. In G. de las Salas, ed. *Proceedings.*
Workshops on Agroforestry Systems in Latin America, Turrialba, Costa Rica.

Vasey, D. E.
1979a   Capybara Ranching in Amazonia? *Oryx* 15(1):47-49.

1979b   Population and Agricultural Intensity in the Humid Tropics. *Human Ecology*
7(3):269-283.

Vayda, A. P. and R. A. Rappaport
1968   Ecology, Cultural and Non-Cultural. In J. A. Clifton, ed. *Introduction to
Cultural Anthropology.* Boston: Houghton Mifflin.

Vermeer, D.
1970   Population Pressure and Crop Rotational Changes Among the Tiv of Nigeria.
Annals of the Association of American Geographers 60:299-314.

Vickers, W. T.
1975   Meat Is Meat: The Siona-Secoya and the Hunting-Prowess-Sexual Reward
Hypothesis. *Latin Americanist* 11(1):1-5.

1976   Cultural Adaptation to Amazonian Habitates: The Siona-Secoya of Ecuador.
Ph.D. Dissertation, University of Florida, Gainesville.

1979   Native Amazonian Subsistence in Diverse Habitats: The Siona-Secoya of
Ecuador. *Studies in Third World Societies* 7:6-36.

1980   An Analysis of Amazonian Hunting Yields as a Function of Settlement Age. In
R. Hames, ed. *Working Papers on South American Indians* #2. Bennington, VT:
Bennington College.

de Voss, A.
1977   Game as Food. *Unasylva* 29(116):2-12.

Wagley, C.
1953   *Amazon Town.* New York: Macmillan.

1969   Cultural Influences on Population: A Comparison of Two Tupi Tribes. In A. P.
Vayda, ed. *Environment and Cultural Behavior.* New York: Natural History
Press.

1974   *Man in the Amazon.* Gainesville: University of Florida Press.

Walker, B. H., ed.
1979   *Management of Semi-Arid Ecosystems.* Amsterdam: Elsevier.

Watson, G. A.
1983   Development of Mixed Tree and Food Crop Systems in the Humid Tropics: A
Response to Population Pressure Deforestation. *Explorations in Agriculture*
19:311-332.

Watters, R. F.
1960   The Nature of Shifting Cultivation: A Review of Recent Research. *Pacific Viewpoint* 1(1):59-99.

1971   *Shifting Cultivation in Latin America.* Forestry Development Paper No. 17.
Rome: FAO.

Wazeka, R.
1982   Bringing Modern Science into Herbal Medicine. *Unasylva* 34(137).

Weinstock, J. A.
1983   Rattan: A Complement to Swidden Agriculture (Borneo). *Economic Botany*
37(1):58-68.

Werner, D. et al.
1979   Subsistence Productivity and Hunting Effort in Native South America. *Human Ecology* 7(4):303-315.

Whitaker, Z. and R. Whitaker
1987   Irulu Tribal Cooperative. *Cultural Survival Quarterly* 11(1):31-33.

Whitten, N. E.
1976   *Sacha Runa: Ethnicity and Adaptation of Ecuadorian Jungle Quichua*. Urbana: University of Illinois Press.

1978   Ecological Imagery and Cultural Adaptability: The Canelos Quichua of Eastern Ecuador. *American Anthropologist* 80(4):836-859.

1981   *Cultural Transformations and Ethnicity in Modern Ecuador*. Urbana: University of Illinois Press.

Wiersum, K. F.
1980   Possibilities for Use and Development of Indigenous Agroforestry Systems for Sustained Land-Use on Java. In J. I. Furtado, ed. *Tropical Ecology and Development*. pp. 515-521. Kuala Lampur: International Society of Tropical Ecology.

1982   Tree Gardening and Taungya in Java: Examples of Agroforestry Techniques in the Humid Tropics. *Agroforestry Systems* 1(1):53-70.

Wiersum, K. F., ed.
1981   *Viewpoints on Agroforestry: A Syllabus of a Lecture Series on Agroforestry*. Wageningen, The Netherlands: Department of Forest Management, Agricultural University.

Wilbert, J., ed.
1961   *The Evolution of Horticultural Systems in Native South America: Causes and Consequences*. Caracas, Venezuela: Sociedad de Ciência Naturales La Salle.

Wilken, G. C.
1969   Drained-Field Agriculture — Intensive Farming System in Tlaxcala, Mexico. *Geographical Review* 59(2):215-241.

1977   Integrating Forest and Small-Scale Farm Systems in Middle America. *Agro-Ecosystems* 3:291-302.

Wilkinson, G. E. et al.
1976   Infiltration of Water into Two Nigerian Soils Under Secondary Forest and Subsequent Arable Cropping. *Geoderma* 15:51-59.

Williams, L.
1960   Little-Known Wealth of Tropical Forests. *Proceedings, Fifth Working Forestry Congress, Seattle* 3:2003-7.

Womersley, J.
1972   Plants, Indigenous Uses. In *Encyclopaedia of Papua and New Guinea*. Vol. II. pp. 908-912. Melbourne, Australia: Melbourne University Press.

Wood, C. and M. Schmink
1979   Blaming the Victim: Small Farmer Production in an Amazonian Colonization Project. *Studies in Third World Societies* 7:77-93.

Wood, R. G.
1971   Agricultural Systems in the Nuba Mountains, Sudan. Dissertation Abstracts International. B 32(7):4006-7.

World Bank
1982   Tribal Peoples and Economic Development. Washington, DC: The World Bank.

Worldwatch
1979   Planting for the Future: Forestry for Human Needs. Washington, DC.

Yantko, J. A. and F. B. Golley
  1977   *World Census of Tropical Ecologists*. Athens, GA: Institute of Ecology.

Yen, D. E.
  1974   Arboriculture in the Subsistence of Santa Cruz, Solomon Islands. *Economic Botany* 28:247-287.

Zanstrata, H.
  n.d.   Field Notes of Research of Multiple Cropping Systems in Tropical Environments. IRRI. Los Banos, the Philippines.

Zarur, G.
  1979   Ecological Need and Cultural Choice in Central Brazil. *Current Anthropology* 20(3):649-653.

About Cultural Survival

Cultural Survival, a nonprofit human rights organization founded in 1972 by social scientists at Harvard University, is concerned with the fate of indigenous peoples and ethnic groups throughout the world. Members include a network of approximately 2,500 anthropologists and other social scientists who have worked with specific groups, particularly indigenous peoples, worldwide. The organization has sponsored and facilitated research on both urgent and chronic issues relating to development and social change in Africa, Latin America and Asia, with a special focus on the general and specific problems confronting indigenous peoples incorporated into encompassing state systems.

Cultural Survival also directly funds projects that are designed and implemented by indigenous peoples themselves to promote their self-sufficiency. This is done with the aim of giving such groups the time and economic resources with which to determine their relation to economic and political systems at the state level.

Cultural Survival often sponsors research, however, on topics in places where it does not have or intend to have in the near future direct assistance projects of its own. One of its purposes as an institution is to make available its own expertise (or the expertise it can rally) to other, larger organizations who either have ongoing programs in areas of concern or have the capacity to launch such programs. Research on the Ethiopian famine fell in line with this latter goal of Cultural Survival.

Research among refugees has become a concern of Cultural Survival in the course of its efforts to protect the rights of indigenous peoples. Racism, discrimination and ethnic persecution in indigenous people's homelands often cause them to cross international borders. Cultural Survival has conducted research among refugees in or from Costa Rica, Djibouti, Ethiopia, Guatemala, Mexico, Nicaragua, Ruanda, Somalia, Sudan and Uganda, and as a result has published numerous documents on the general relationship between ethnicity and refugee status.

Recently, Cultural Survival has begun to evaluate resource management projects run by indigenous peoples and funded by Cultural Survival as well as other organizations.

Cultural Survival publishes and/or distributes more than 350 documents about the plight of indigenous peoples and ethnic minorities throughout the world.

CULTURAL SURVIVAL PUBLICATIONS
CULTURAL SURVIVAL REPORTS

Politics and the Ethiopian Famine, 1984–1985. By Jason W. Clay and Bonnie K. Holcomb. (No. 20, December 1986; revised edition.) 240 pages. $9.95.

Southeast Asian Tribal Groups and Ethnic Minorities. Proceedings of a Cultural Survival-sponsored conference. (No. 22, 1988.) $10.

Coca and Cocaine: Effects on People and Policy in Latin America. Edited by Deborah Pacini and Christine Franquemont. Proceedings of the conference "The Coca Leaf and Its Derivatives — Biology, Society and Policy." Published with the Latin American Studies Program, Cornell University. (No. 23, June 1986.) 169 pages. $8.

Human Rights and Anthropology. Edited by Theodore E. Downing and Gilbert Kushner, with Human Rights Internet. (No. 24, 1988.) 208 pages. $12.

The Spoils of Famine: Ethiopian Famine Policy and Peasant Agriculture. By Jason W. Clay, Sandra Steingraber and Peter Niggli. (No. 25, 1988.) 200 pages. $15.

A Sea of Small Boats. Edited by John Cordell. (No. 26, 1988.) 300 pages. $12.95.

Indigenous Peoples and Tropical Forests: Models of Land Use and Management from Latin America. By Jason W. Clay. (No. 27, 1988.) 150 pages. $7.

Report from the Frontier: The State of the World's Indigenous Peoples. By Julian Burger. (No. 28, 1987.) 320 pages. $15.

(Cultural Survival Reports continue the Occasional Paper series.)

OCCASIONAL PAPERS

The Chinese Exodus from Vietnam: Implications for the Southeast Asian Chinese. By Judith Strauch. (No. 1, December 1980.) 15 pages. $1.50.

East Timor: Five Years After the Indonesian Invasion. Statements by M. Alkatiri, R. Clark, J. Dunn, J. Joliffe, Amnesty International, E. Traube and B. R. O'G. Anderson to the Fourth Committee of the U.N. General Assembly; articles by D. Southerland (*The Christian Science Monitor*) and T. Harkin (*The Progressive*). (No. 2, January 1981.) 42 pages. $2.25.

The Cerro Colorado Copper Project and the Guaymí Indians of Panama. By Chris N. Gjording, S. J. (No. 3, March 1981.) 50 pages. $2.50.

The Akawaio, the Upper Mazaruni Hydroelectric Project, and National Development in Guyana. By William Henningsgaard. (No. 4, June 1981.) 37 pages. $2.

Brazilian Indians Under the Law. Proceedings of a Cultural Survival-sponsored conference of lawyers and anthropologists in Santa Catarina, Brazil, in October 1980. (No. 5, September 1981.) 14 pages. $1.25.

In the Path of Polonoroeste: Endangered Peoples of Western Brazil. Articles by D. Maybury-Lewis, D. Price, D. Moore, C. Junqueira, B. M. Lafer and J. Clay. (No. 6, September 1981.) 66 pages. $2.75.

The Plight of Peripheral People in Papua New Guinea. Volume I: The Inland Situation. Edited by Robert Gordon. Contributions by J. Flanagan, P. Huber, D. Jorgenson, J.-C. Martin and F.-R. Ouellette, N. L. Maclean, and E. L. Schieffelin. (No. 7, October 1981.) 95 pages. $5.

The Dialectics of Domination in Peru: Native Communities and the Myth of the Vast Amazonian Emptiness. By Richard Chase Smith. (No. 8, October 1982.) 131 pages. $6.

The San in Transition. Volume I: A Guide to "N!ai, the Story of a !Kung Woman." By Toby Alice Volkman. Published with Documentary Education Resources. (No. 9, November 1982.) 56 pages. $2.50.

Voices of the Survivors. The Massacre at Finca San Francisco, Guatemala. Published with the Anthropology Resource Center. (No. 10, September 1983.) 105 pages. $5.

The Impact of Contact: Two Yanomama Case Studies. By John Saffirio & Raymond Hames, and Napoleon Chagnon & Thomas F. Melancon. Published with Working Papers on South America. (No. 11, November 1983.) 66 pages. $4.

Micronesia as Strategic Colony: The Impact of U.S. Policy on Micronesian Health and Culture. Edited by Catherine Lutz. (No. 12, June 1984.) 109 pages. $6.

The San in Transition, Volume II: What Future for the Ju/Wasi of Nyae-Nyae? By Robert Gordon. (No. 13, July 1984.) 44 pages. $2.50.

The Eviction of Banyaruanda: The Story Behind the Refugee Crisis in Southwest Uganda. By Jason W. Clay. (No. 14, August 1984.) 77 pages. $4.

Resource Development and Indigenous People: The El Cerrejón Coal Project and the Guajiro of Colombia. By Deborah Pacini Hernandez. (No. 15, November 1984.) 54 pages. $3.50.

Native Peoples and Economic Development: Six Case Studies from Latin America. Edited by Theodore Macdonald, Jr. (No. 16, December 1984.) 103 pages. $6.50.

Art, Knowledge and Health: Development and Assessment of a Collaborative Auto-Financed Organization in Eastern Ecuador. By Dorothea S. Whitten and Norman Whitten, Jr. Published with the Sacha Runa Research Foundation. (No. 17, January 1985.) 126 pages. $7.

The Future of Former Foragers in Australia and Southern Africa. Edited by Carmel Schrire and Robert Gordon. (No. 18, October 1985.) 125 pages. $8.

Ethnic Diversity on a Corporate Plantation: Guaymí Labor on a United Brands Subsidiary in Costa Rica and Panama. By Philippe Bourgois. (No. 19, December 1985.) 52 pages. $4.

Strategies and Conditions of Political and Cultural Survival in American Indian Societies. By Duane Champagne. (No. 21, December 1985.) 56 pages. $5.

SPECIAL REPORTS

Brazil. Articles translated from "A Questão de Emancipação" (Comissão Pro-Indio, São Paulo, 1979) and "Nimuendaju" (Comissão Pro-Indio, Rio de Janeiro, 1979). (No. 1, December 1979.) 68 pages. $1.

The Indian Peoples of Paraguay: Their Plight and Their Prospects. By David Maybury-Lewis and James Howe. (No. 2, October 1980.) 122 pages. $4.

Amazonía Ecuatoriana: La Otra Cara del Progreso. Edited by Norman E. Whitten, Jr. Contributions by N. E. Whitten, Jr., E. Salazar, P. Descola, A. C. Taylor, W. Belzner, T. Macdonald, Jr., and D. Whitten. Published with Mundo Shuar. (No. 3, 1981.) 227 pages. $2.50.

Fishers of Men or Founders of Empire? The Wycliffe Bible Translators in Latin America. A U.S. Evangelical Mission in the Third World. By David Stoll. Published with Zed Press. (No. 4, December 1982.) 344 pages. $12.99.

Add $2 postage and handling charge for all orders of three titles or less. After three titles, add 50¢ for each additional book. Titles not yet published or out of stock will be backordered and shipped as soon as they are available. Please send check or money order for the amount of order to Cultural Survival Publications, 11 Divinity Avenue, Cambridge, MA 02138. Bookstores and those needing publications for classroom use should write for special rates.